SHI ZHI HUI

How to Master Yourself

Master Shi Heng Yi's Guide to Self-Discovery and Inner Strength

This book was professionally typeset on Reedsy.
Find out more at reedsy.com

Contents

Introduction

I still remember the night I received the call. It was just past midnight, and the voice on the other end belonged to Michael, a friend I'd known since college. His words came in broken fragments, punctuated by long silences that said more than his actual speech. He had just walked away from his third job in two years. His relationship had collapsed. He was living in a sparse apartment with boxes he hadn't unpacked in months. "I don't know who I am anymore," he confessed. "I keep chasing things I think will make me happy, but nothing sticks. I'm just... drifting."

As I listened to Michael describe his life-a constant cycle of new beginnings that somehow always led back to the same emptiness-I recognized a pattern that has become increasingly common in our world of endless choices and constant distraction. Here was a man with talent, education, and opportunity, yet he felt fundamentally lost, unable to find solid ground or lasting purpose.

In the days that followed our conversation, I couldn't stop thinking about Michael's situation. It wasn't just about career indecision or relationship troubles-it was about something deeper: a disconnection from himself, an inability to recognize his own patterns, and a lack of the inner framework needed to navigate life's challenges with clarity and purpose.

And Michael wasn't alone. I began noticing this same struggle in colleagues burning out despite outward success, in friends who seemed perpetually dissatisfied despite changing all the external circumstances of their lives, and in the broader cultural conversation about meaning, purpose, and mental well-being.

It was during this period of reflection that I recalled my encounters with Master Shi Heng Yi, the 35th-generation Shaolin master whose wisdom has touched millions through his teachings on self-mastery and inner peace. I remembered watching him break bricks not through brute strength, but through focused intention and complete presence-a physical demonstration of the mind-body unity he embodies.

What struck me most about Master Shi Heng Yi's approach was how he translated ancient Shaolin wisdom into practical guidance for modern life. He didn't advocate escaping from the world's challenges but offered tools to face them with greater awareness, discipline, and inner stability. His message wasn't about achieving perfection but about continuous refinement-learning to recognize our patterns, overcome our internal obstacles, and cultivate the virtues that form the foundation of a meaningful life.

The more I reflected on Michael's struggles and Master Shi Heng Yi's teachings, the clearer it became that what many of us lack isn't more information or more options-it's a framework for self-understanding and self-mastery. We've outsourced our well-being to external circumstances, forgotten how to use our bodies as they were intended, and lost touch with the inner compass that guides us through life's complexity.

This realization was the seed from which this book grew. Drawing on Master Shi Heng Yi's profound insights and practical wisdom, I wanted to create a guide for anyone feeling lost, stuck, or disconnected-a pathway back to themselves and forward to greater purpose and peace.

In the pages that follow, you'll discover how to identify and overcome the five hindrances that block your progress, how to break free from limiting patterns, how to build character through the cultivation of virtue, and how to find lasting purpose and peace in a world of constant change. You'll learn practical tools like the RAIN method for working with difficult emotions, standing practices for building willpower, and daily routines that foster greater awareness and presence.

This book isn't about quick fixes or surface-level solutions. It's about the journey of becoming your own master-taking responsibility for your mind and body, developing the discipline and awareness needed to navigate life's challenges, and connecting with the deeper source of meaning that lies within you.

My hope is that this book serves as both a mirror and a map-reflecting back to you your own patterns and potential, while offering clear guidance for the path ahead. Whether you're feeling lost like my friend Michael, seeking greater purpose and meaning, or simply wanting to refine your approach to life's challenges, the wisdom of Master Shi Heng Yi offers a timeless and practical path forward.

The journey to self-mastery isn't always easy, but it is always worthwhile. As Master Shi Heng Yi teaches, "The master is already sitting inside of each individual. It's just that we don't nourish that master inside of us enough." May this book help you recognize and nourish the master within.

I

The Foundations of Self-Mastery

Explore the modern challenges of choice overload, disconnection from body and mind, and the importance of self-reflection. Learn why structure, discipline, and a clear sense of purpose are essential starting points for the journey toward self-mastery

.

1

The Modern Struggle-Why Self-Mastery Matters

In my years working with people from all walks of life-from corporate executives to spiritual seekers-I've witnessed a profound paradox unfold. Despite unprecedented access to information, technology, and opportunity, more people feel lost, anxious, and disconnected than ever before. This observation first struck me during a retreat I led for high-performing professionals who, by conventional standards, had "made it." Yet in private conversations, they confessed to feeling empty, overwhelmed, and uncertain about their direction.

This modern struggle is precisely what drew me to Master Shi Heng Yi's teachings. His insights, rooted in ancient Shaolin wisdom yet perfectly calibrated for our contemporary challenges, offer a pathway through the maze of modern existence. As he explains, "This world is filled with so much choice that it's difficult to take a decision which direction to go, what is right to do."

The abundance of choice in our modern world has created what psychologists call "choice overload" or "decision fatigue." When faced with too many options, we often delay making decisions, sometimes indefinitely. We make poorer choices than we would with fewer options. We feel less satisfied with our selections, even when they're objectively good. And perhaps most significantly, we experience heightened anxiety and stress.

I recall working with a talented professional who spent three years contemplating a career change. She had spreadsheets analyzing different industries, salary projections, and potential satisfaction levels. Yet the more data she gathered, the more paralyzed she became. "I have too many options," she told me. "How can I possibly know which is right?"

This paralysis isn't just inconvenient-it's life-diminishing. While we deliberate, life passes us by. As Master Shi Heng Yi teaches, we become trapped in a cycle of perpetual seeking without finding, constantly searching for the perfect option that may not exist.

Perhaps even more concerning than our decision paralysis is our growing disconnection from our physical selves. Master Shi Heng Yi observes: "Whoever created us did not create us to sit with our butt on one place and do thinking work the whole time."

Our bodies evolved for movement, for physical engagement with our environment. Yet modern life has engineered physical activity out of our daily existence. We sit for hours daily. We communicate through screens rather than face-to-face interaction. We outsource physical labor to machines and services. We experience nature primarily through digital representations.

This sedentary existence creates what Master Shi Heng Yi calls "unbalanced energies" in the body. These manifest as restlessness, anxiety, and a vague but persistent sense that something is missing. Our bodies, designed for movement and physical challenge, signal their distress through these symptoms.

Equally concerning is our mental disconnection. Despite-or perhaps because of-constant digital stimulation, we've lost the ability to be present with our own thoughts. We check our phones dozens of times daily. We consume information constantly but rarely digest it. We communicate continuously but seldom connect deeply.

When we combine choice overload with physical and mental disconnection, we find ourselves living on autopilot-moving through life without conscious direction or presence. The costs of this unconscious existence are steep.

Without awareness, we miss the richness of experience. Meals become fuel rather than pleasure. Conversations become transactions rather than connections. Achievements become checkboxes rather than sources of genuine fulfillment.

Without awareness, we repeat the same patterns-in relationships, career decisions, and personal habits-expecting different results. I've worked with countless individuals who find themselves in the same dysfunctional relationship dynamics or career dead-ends, wondering how they arrived there yet again.

The physical toll of disconnection manifests in rising rates of chronic disease, obesity, and mental health challenges. Our bodies cannot sustain prolonged disconnection without consequence.

Perhaps most profoundly, living on autopilot leads to what philosophers call "existential emptiness"-a sense that life lacks meaning or purpose. This emptiness often surfaces at midlife or during major transitions, when external achievements no longer satisfy our deeper needs for meaning and connection.

A senior executive I worked with described this emptiness perfectly: "I climbed the ladder only to discover it was leaning against the wrong wall. Now I'm at the top, and I don't know where to go next or why I wanted to be here in the first place."

This is why self-mastery matters now more than ever. In a world designed to capture and monetize our attention, taking conscious control of our focus, choices, and actions isn't just beneficial-it's essential for a life of meaning and fulfillment.

As Master Shi Heng Yi teaches, the path to freedom begins with awareness-recognizing our current state without judgment. Only then can we begin the journey toward greater presence, purpose, and peace.

Notes

Day:
Date & Month:

2

The Nature of Self-Knowing Yourself

Early in my training with Master Shi Heng Yi, he posed a question that still resonates with me: "If you don't know who you are, how can you possibly know what you need?" This simple inquiry cuts to the heart of our modern predicament. Many of us move through life pursuing goals, relationships, and experiences without a fundamental understanding of ourselves-our true nature, values, and purpose.

Master Shi Heng Yi emphasizes this understanding as the foundation of all meaningful growth: "If you have the wrong perspective of who you are, what you are, everything else in this lifetime you base your decisions on is just not going to be placed in the right direction."

Self-knowledge begins with self-reflection-the willingness to look inward with honesty and courage. Yet genuine self-reflection has become increasingly rare in our distracted world. We fill every moment with noise, activity, and information, leaving no space for the quiet contemplation that nurtures self-awareness.

Master Shi Heng Yi recommends regular periods of silence and

13

stillness-what he calls "sitting practice"-as essential for developing self-knowledge. This doesn't require formal meditation (though that can be valuable). It simply means creating space in your day to be with yourself, to observe your thoughts, emotions, and physical sensations without judgment or distraction.

Start with just five minutes daily. Sit comfortably, close your eyes, and simply notice what arises in your awareness. Don't try to control or change your experience-just observe it with curiosity. Over time, extend this practice to 10, 15, or 20 minutes.

Through this simple practice, patterns begin to emerge. You may notice recurring thoughts, emotional tendencies, or physical tensions that reveal deeper aspects of yourself. These observations form the basis of honest self-assessment.

Self-assessment requires asking difficult questions about what patterns keep repeating in your life, what triggers strong emotional reactions in you and why, what values you claim to hold and whether your actions align with them, and what you might be avoiding or denying about yourself.

I've found that maintaining a reflective journal accelerates this process. Writing crystallizes thoughts that might otherwise remain vague or unexamined. One executive I worked with discovered through journaling that her chronic job dissatisfaction stemmed not from the work itself but from a deeper pattern of seeking her father's approval through achievement-a pattern that no career success could satisfy.

This honest self-assessment isn't always comfortable. We all maintain self-protective illusions that can be painful to relinquish. Yet as Master Shi Heng Yi teaches, true freedom comes only through facing ourselves with complete honesty.

One of Master Shi Heng Yi's most powerful metaphors is that of the director and the actor. Most of us, he suggests, are so immersed in playing our role that we forget we're also the director of our life's movie.

"Jump out of the body and watch yourself right now," he advises. "You are sitting… and you are writing your story. How do you want to write the story?"

This shift in perspective-from actor to director-creates psychological distance that enables clearer seeing and wiser choices. Rather than being swept along by events and reactions, we can pause, step back, and consider what story we are currently living, if this is the story we want to write, what character we are playing and if this is who we truly are, and how we might direct this scene differently.

I've seen this perspective shift transform lives. A physician I coached was caught in a narrative of martyrdom-overworking, sacrificing her health and relationships for her patients, and growing increasingly resentful. When she "stepped into the director's chair" and examined this story, she realized it wasn't serving anyone-not her patients, her family, or herself. From this new perspective, she could write a different story-one of balanced service, self-care, and sustainable compassion.

This director's perspective also helps us distinguish between our essential self and the various roles we play. We are not merely our job title, relationship status, or social identity. These are roles in our life's movie, but they don't define our deeper nature. When we confuse role with identity, we become vulnerable to crisis when roles change through job loss, relationship endings, or other transitions.

A crucial aspect of self-knowledge is understanding our relationship with time. Many of us live primarily in the future-planning, worrying, and striving toward goals that always remain just beyond reach. Others dwell in the past-replaying old hurts, glorifying former achievements, or wishing for what might have been.

Master Shi Heng Yi teaches the importance of balancing future vision with present reality: "How do you balance out vision with reality? The only thing real right now is this."

This balance doesn't mean abandoning goals or forgetting the lessons of the past. Rather, it means holding these perspectives lightly while remaining grounded in the present moment-the only point where life actually happens and choices can be made.

Achieving this balance requires recognizing when we've tilted too far in either direction. Signs of future-fixation include persistent anxiety about what might happen, difficulty enjoying current achievements or experiences, constantly moving goalposts for satisfaction, and the feeling that life will begin "when I achieve X." Signs of past-fixation include ruminating on regrets or past injuries, comparing present circumstances unfavorably to the past, inability to adapt to current realities, and defining yourself primarily by past roles or achievements.

The balanced perspective acknowledges that while we can learn from the past and plan for the future, we can only act in the present. As Master Shi Heng Yi reminds us, "We don't know if we wake up tomorrow." This isn't meant to induce fear but to awaken us to the preciousness of now.

I've found that regular "present moment check-ins" help maintain this balance. Several times daily, pause and ask where your attention is right now-past, present, or future, what is actually happening in this moment, and what you can appreciate about right now.

The journey of self-knowledge is ongoing-we never arrive at complete understanding. Yet even small increases in self-awareness yield profound benefits. As we come to know ourselves more deeply, our choices align more naturally with our true nature, our relationships become more authentic, and our sense of purpose emerges with greater clarity.

In the words of Master Shi Heng Yi: "The only thing you need to do is look at yourself right now and just find out what is it that makes you unhappy... And this is the same question for everyone. But what you ultimately need to tackle is different."

This individualized approach to self-knowledge honors the unique journey each of us must undertake. There is no standardized map, only the compass of honest self-reflection and the courage to follow where it leads.

Notes

Day:
Date & Month:

3

The Power of Structure and Discipline

When I first encountered Master Shi Heng Yi's teachings on discipline and structure, I was struck by how radically they differed from popular notions of freedom. In a world that often equates freedom with unlimited choice and the absence of constraints, his perspective offers a revolutionary alternative: discipline is not the opposite of freedom but its prerequisite.

The word "discipline" often evokes negative associations-punishment, restriction, denial of pleasure. Yet its Latin root, disciplina, simply means "teaching" or "learning." True discipline is not imposed from outside but cultivated from within as we align our actions with our deeper values and aspirations.

Master Shi Heng Yi describes discipline as the capacity to direct our energy consciously rather than being driven by momentary impulses, external pressures, or habitual patterns. This capacity creates freedom in several dimensions.

Without discipline, we become slaves to our fluctuating desires, emotions, and thoughts. The craving for immediate gratification overrides our longer-term interests. The executive who can't resist checking email during family dinner, the student who abandons studying for social media, the dieter who consistently surrenders to momentary cravings-all experience the subtle tyranny of undisciplined impulses.

Meaningful achievements require sustained effort over time. Whether building a business, mastering a craft, raising children, or developing spiritual insight, the path is rarely smooth or continuously rewarding. Discipline provides the bridge over inevitable periods of difficulty, boredom, or doubt.

In an attention economy designed to capture and monetize our focus, the undisciplined mind becomes easily manipulated. Companies invest billions in understanding the psychology of distraction and habit formation. Discipline serves as a protective barrier, allowing us to engage with technology and media on our terms rather than being unconsciously driven by algorithms designed to maximize engagement.

I've witnessed this freedom through discipline most powerfully in a former client-a creative professional who struggled with severe ADHD. His days were chaotic, his projects perpetually unfinished, his relationships strained by unreliability. Through gradually implementing structured routines and disciplined practices, he discovered an unexpected liberation. "For the first time," he told me, "I'm free to create what matters to me instead of being hijacked by every passing thought or distraction."

If discipline is the capacity to direct energy consciously, structure provides the framework that supports this direction. Structure includes routines, systems, boundaries, and practices that align our daily actions with our deeper intentions.

Master Shi Heng Yi's own life exemplifies this principle. His morning begins with silence, conscious breathing, and standing practice-a

21

structure that creates space for presence before the day's demands. This structure doesn't constrain his freedom; it creates the conditions for deeper freedom to emerge.

Effective structure serves several functions. It conserves decision energy by creating routines for recurring activities. Every decision depletes our limited daily reserve of willpower. By creating routines for recurring activities (when to wake, what to eat, when to exercise, etc.), we conserve decision energy for truly important choices.

Structure creates protective boundaries in a world of endless demands and distractions. These might include technology boundaries (no phones during meals), time boundaries (work hours that don't encroach on family time), or personal boundaries (learning to say no to commitments that don't align with core values).

Our physical and social environments powerfully influence our behavior, often below conscious awareness. Structuring these environments to support rather than undermine our intentions is a crucial form of self-mastery. This might mean removing temptations, surrounding ourselves with supportive relationships, or creating spaces conducive to focused work or relaxation.

I've found that the most effective structures balance consistency with flexibility. Too rigid, and structure becomes brittle, unable to adapt to changing circumstances. Too loose, and it fails to provide the necessary support for discipline. The art lies in creating what I call "flexible firmness"-clear structures with built-in adaptability.

One executive I worked with established a firm morning routine (wake at 5:30, meditate for 20 minutes, exercise for 30) but built in flexibility about the specific form of exercise based on energy levels and weather. This balance allowed the structure to persist through travel, seasonal changes, and varying work demands.

Master Shi Heng Yi emphasizes that self-mastery emerges not from occasional heroic efforts but from consistent small actions: "It's not helpful to like six days per week do nothing and then you go one day to the gym and give your everything. No, it's better you have some type of consistency throughout the whole day. This is what builds patterns, healthy patterns."

Our lives are largely shaped by habits-automated behaviors that require minimal conscious attention. Research suggests that up to 45% of our daily actions are habitual rather than consciously chosen. These habits, for better or worse, compound over time to create our health, relationships, career trajectories, and overall well-being.

The power of habits lies in their cumulative effect. Reading 20 pages daily equals 30+ books annually. Saving $10 daily accumulates to $3,650 yearly plus compound interest. A daily 10-minute meditation practice totals 60+ hours of mindfulness training yearly. Consuming 100 extra calories daily leads to 10+ pounds of weight gain annually.

Small actions, consistently applied, create dramatic results over time- a principle Master Shi Heng Yi embodies through his decades of daily practice.

Developing effective habits involves understanding three key components: the trigger, the routine, and the reward. Every habit begins with a cue or trigger-a time of day, emotional state, location, preceding action, or social context that initiates the behavior. By consciously designing triggers for desired habits, we can make positive behaviors more automatic.

The routine is the habit itself-the behavior or action that follows the trigger. Starting with "tiny habits" increases the likelihood of consistency. Begin with just one minute of meditation, one paragraph of writing, or one push-up. Once the habit is established, gradually extend the duration or intensity.

Habits persist because they're rewarding, either inherently or through artificial reinforcement. Identifying and enhancing the rewards of positive habits accelerates their development. This might involve celebrating small wins, tracking progress visually, or pairing a challenging habit with something immediately pleasurable.

I've found that habit "stacking"-attaching a new habit to an established one-significantly increases success rates. A client who struggled to establish a meditation practice finally succeeded by linking it to his existing coffee ritual: boiling water for coffee became the trigger for a three-minute meditation while the water heated.

Master Shi Heng Yi reminds us that the quality of our habits ultimately shapes the quality of our character: "The virtues are building the framework of the character." By consciously cultivating habits aligned with our deeper values and aspirations, we gradually become the person capable of living the life we envision.

This is perhaps the most profound freedom that discipline and structure offer-the freedom to shape ourselves from within, to direct our own development rather than being formed by default through unconscious patterns and external influences.

As we conclude this exploration of the foundations of self-mastery, remember that the journey begins not with grand transformations but with small, consistent steps. By understanding the modern challenges we face, developing deeper self-knowledge, and embracing the power of discipline and structure, we lay the groundwork for lasting change.

In the words of Master Shi Heng Yi: "The master is already sitting inside of each individual. It's just that we don't nourish that master inside of us enough." The practices and principles we've explored are not about becoming someone different but about uncovering and nourishing the master that already exists within each of us.

Notes

Day:
Date & Month:

II

The Five Hindrances-Identifying Your Inner Obstacles

Discover the five mental states-sensual desire, ill will, dullness, restlessness, and self-doubt-that block progress. Learn to recognize these patterns in your life and understand how they undermine your goals and personal growth

.

4

The Five Hindrances Explained

In my years of studying both Eastern wisdom traditions and modern psychology, few frameworks have proven as universally applicable as Master Shi Heng Yi's teachings on the Five Hindrances. I first encountered these concepts during a particularly challenging period in my corporate career, when despite outward success, I felt fundamentally stuck-unable to progress toward my deeper goals and aspirations.

It was during a retreat at the Shaolin Temple Europe that Master Shi Heng Yi explained these hindrances not as abstract philosophical concepts, but as practical, observable mental states that we all experience. What struck me most was how these ancient teachings perfectly described the very obstacles I was facing in my modern life.

The Five Hindrances represent different states of mind that make it difficult to see clearly and therefore engage in right decisions. They are the primary blocks to our progress-not just in meditation or spiritual practice, but in any goal we set for ourselves. Whether you're aiming to advance in your career, improve your relationships, or simply find greater peace and purpose, these hindrances will inevitably arise.

Sensual Desire: The Pull of Pleasure and Distraction

The first hindrance, sensual desire, arises when we become overly receptive to pleasurable sensations through our five senses: seeing, hearing, smelling, tasting, and feeling. Master Shi Heng Yi describes it beautifully through the metaphor of climbing a mountain:

"So in your mind, you climb up that mountain. After one mile of walking, you discover a beautiful restaurant surrounded by beautiful people. You smell delicious food and the great variety of beverages. When you follow that temptation, you have already lost your track."

This hindrance isn't limited to obvious pleasures like food or physical comfort. In our digital age, it manifests most commonly as the endless stream of notifications, social media updates, and entertainment options that constantly vie for our attention. Each ping, each scroll, each click offers a small dopamine hit-a momentary pleasure that pulls us away from our deeper intentions.

I've witnessed this countless times in my coaching practice. A client commits to working on an important project, only to find themselves checking email "just for a minute," which turns into an hour of responding to non-urgent messages. Another sets aside time for strategic thinking but gets pulled into the pleasure of solving immediate, less important problems because the quick wins feel good.

When sensual desire becomes particularly strong, it transforms into obsession. We don't just get momentarily distracted-we become unable to pull ourselves away from the source of pleasure. Think of the executive who can't stop checking work emails during family dinner, the student who abandons studying for the instant gratification of social media, or the writer who never finishes their book because they keep getting pulled into researching interesting but tangential topics.

The key insight about sensual desire is that it's not about denying pleasure-it's about recognizing when the pursuit of pleasure is pulling us off our chosen path. As Master Shi Heng Yi teaches, remaining at that metaphorical restaurant means you can't continue your journey up the mountain. The momentary pleasure comes at the cost of your deeper goals.

Ill Will/Aversion: Resistance to Discomfort and Challenge

The second hindrance, ill will or aversion, represents the opposite pull. Rather than being drawn toward pleasure, we push away discomfort, challenge, or anything we dislike. Master Shi Heng Yi explains:

"You are climbing the mountain, and it starts to rain. But you don't like rain. You discover the roads are bumpy, but you don't like bumpy roads. In order to cross the river, you need to swim. But you don't like swimming. Whatever it is that you dislike, it won't make it a pleasant journey."

In psychological terms, this is often called experiential avoidance-actively trying to avoid certain experiences, whether they're external challenges or internal states like uncomfortable emotions or thoughts.

I've experienced this hindrance acutely in my own journey. After leaving a prestigious but unfulfilling corporate position to pursue more meaningful work, I found myself avoiding the discomfort of uncertainty. Each time I faced a challenge-a rejected proposal, a difficult conversation, a period of financial instability-my mind would generate reasons to retreat to safer, more comfortable territory.

Ill will manifests in countless ways in our daily lives: procrastinating on difficult tasks, avoiding necessary but uncomfortable conversations, refusing to engage with perspectives that challenge our own, or even rejecting physical discomfort through excessive comfort-seeking. It's the voice that says, "I'll work on that when I feel more motivated" or "I can't possibly focus in this noisy environment" or "I'll start my fitness routine when the weather improves."

The cost of this hindrance is profound. As Master Shi Heng Yi notes, "Unless you learn to let go of this ill will, it's more likely even that you won't continue that journey." The path to any worthwhile goal inevitably includes discomfort, challenge, and things we'd rather avoid. When we allow aversion to guide our choices, we abandon our deeper aspirations for the temporary relief of avoiding discomfort.

Dullness/Sloth: Lack of Motivation and Energy

The third hindrance is traditionally translated as "sloth and torpor," which Master Shi Heng Yi describes as "the heaviness of the body and the dullness of the mind." This state is characterized by sleepiness, lack of motivation, low energy, and sometimes even depression.

He uses a powerful metaphor for this hindrance: "A simile used in Buddhism describes it as imprisonment. You find yourself locked in a cell. It becomes very hard to make any type of mental or physical effort."

This hindrance is particularly challenging because unlike the previous two, which involve active engagement (either pulling toward pleasure or pushing away discomfort), dullness is passive. It's the foggy, heavy feeling that makes even getting started seem impossible.

I recall working with a talented artist who struggled with this hindrance. Despite genuine passion for her craft, she would describe feeling as though her body was made of lead whenever she approached her studio. "I know exactly what I want to create," she told me, "but it's like there's a wall between knowing and doing that I just can't break through."

In our achievement-oriented culture, we often misinterpret this hindrance as laziness or lack of willpower. But Master Shi Heng Yi's teachings reveal a deeper understanding: dullness is a mental state that can arise for anyone, regardless of their usual level of motivation or discipline. It may be triggered by physical factors like poor sleep or nutrition, emotional factors like burnout or grief, or even existential factors like lack of meaning or purpose.

The only way forward, as Master Shi Heng Yi teaches, is to "find a way to get out from that hole, from that cell." This requires recognizing the state for what it is-not a permanent character flaw, but a temporary hindrance that can be worked with skillfully.

Restlessness: Inability to Focus on the Present

The fourth hindrance, restlessness, represents the opposite of dullness. Rather than being too sluggish, the mind becomes too agitated to settle in the present moment. Master Shi Heng Yi describes it as "the state of an unsettled mind" that is "either worrying about the future or traveling into the past and rejecting, judging about an event that happened in your past."

He uses the vivid metaphor of the "monkey mind"-constantly jumping from one branch to another, unable to stay in one place for long. This restlessness prevents clarity because "there is no time to see clearly anymore."

This hindrance is perhaps the most prevalent in our modern world. With constant digital connectivity, endless to-do lists, and a culture that celebrates busyness, many of us live in a perpetual state of mental agitation. We check our phones while waiting in line, fill every moment with podcasts or music, and feel anxious when faced with silence or stillness.

I've worked with countless executives who pride themselves on their ability to multitask and stay busy, only to realize that this constant activity masks a deeper inability to be present and focused. One CEO I coached tracked his attention for a week and was shocked to discover that he rarely spent more than three minutes on any single task without switching to something else.

The cost of restlessness is subtle but severe. Without the ability to settle our attention on what's in front of us, we miss opportunities, overlook important details, and make decisions based on partial information. Perhaps most significantly, we miss the depth and richness of our own lives as we're perpetually rushing to the next moment.

Skeptical Doubt: Indecision and Lack of Self-Trust

The fifth and final hindrance is skeptical doubt, which Master Shi Heng Yi describes as "very closely related to a state of mind which is based on indecisiveness." In this state, we get "lost in thoughts" of questioning and second-guessing: "Can I do this? Is this the right path? What will the others say? What if this? What if that?"

The result is that "the mind cannot synchronize with your own actions anymore," creating a disconnect between our goals and aspirations and our ability to act on them. As Master Shi Heng Yi observes, "When the way is filled with too much doubts, more often you will stop instead of moving on."

This hindrance manifests as the paralysis of analysis-researching endlessly without taking action, seeking more and more opinions before making a decision, or constantly questioning whether you're on the right path. It's the voice that whispers, "Who am I to do this?" or "What if I make the wrong choice?" or "I need to be 100% certain before I proceed."

I experienced this hindrance acutely when writing this very book. Despite years of studying Master Shi Heng Yi's teachings and seeing their transformative impact in my own life and the lives of my clients, doubt would creep in: "Who am I to interpret these ancient teachings? What if I get something wrong? What if readers don't find value in my perspective?"

What makes skeptical doubt particularly insidious is that it can masquerade as wisdom or prudence. We tell ourselves we're being thorough, careful, or thoughtful, when in reality, we're simply afraid to commit to a direction. As Master Shi Heng Yi teaches, this doubt disconnects us "from the goals and aspirations that once you have set to yourself."

These five hindrances-sensual desire, ill will, dullness, restlessness, and skeptical doubt-are not personal failings or character flaws. They are universal human experiences, mental states that arise for all of us at different times. The key to working with them, as we'll explore in the following chapters, lies first in recognizing them when they appear, and then applying skillful methods to prevent them from blocking our path.

Notes

Day:
Date & Month:

5

How the Hindrances Block Your Path

Understanding the five hindrances conceptually is one thing; recognizing how they operate in your daily life is quite another. In my years of working with individuals across various contexts-from corporate executives to spiritual seekers, from young professionals to retirees-I've observed how these hindrances manifest in countless ways, often so subtly that we don't recognize their influence until they've already derailed our progress.

In this chapter, we'll explore concrete examples of the hindrances at work, examine the relationship between these mental states and our suffering, and develop the capacity to recognize our own patterns. For it is only by seeing clearly how these hindrances operate in our lives that we can begin to work with them skillfully.

Real-life Examples of the Hindrances at Work

Let's begin with sensual desire, the first hindrance. Consider Sarah, a marketing executive I coached who was determined to launch her own consulting business. She had the skills, the network, and a solid business plan. Yet month after month, her launch date kept getting pushed back. When we examined her daily patterns, we discovered that each time she sat down to work on her business, she would first "quickly check" her email or social media. These momentary pleasures would inevitably lead to hours of distraction.

"It's like I'm addicted to the little dopamine hits," she admitted. "Even though I genuinely want to build my business, in the moment, the immediate gratification of responding to messages or scrolling through updates feels more compelling than the harder work of building something from scratch."

Sarah's experience illustrates how sensual desire operates-not as a conscious rejection of our goals, but as a subtle pull toward immediate pleasure that gradually takes us off course. The key insight for Sarah came when she realized this wasn't a character flaw but a predictable hindrance that she could learn to work with.

Ill will or aversion manifests just as commonly but in the opposite direction. Take Michael, a talented programmer who dreamed of creating his own app. Unlike Sarah, Michael had no trouble avoiding distractions. His challenge was facing the inevitable difficulties of development.

"Every time I hit a coding problem I can't immediately solve, I find myself getting frustrated and switching to a different part of the project," he explained. "As a result, I have a dozen half-finished features and nothing that actually works end-to-end."

Michael's aversion to the discomfort of being stuck-of not knowing the answer right away-was preventing him from making meaningful progress. His story illustrates how ill will doesn't just apply to obvious dislikes (such as physical discomfort or unpleasant tasks) but to any experience we resist, including the natural challenges that arise on any worthwhile path.

Dullness or sloth often shows up as a mysterious lack of energy for things we genuinely care about. Elena, a writer I worked with, described it this way: "I have all these ideas I'm excited about, but when I actually sit down to write, it's like someone pulled the plug on my energy. Even opening my laptop feels like lifting a hundred pounds."

What made this particularly confusing for Elena was that she had no trouble finding energy for other activities, like exercising or socializing. It was specifically when facing her most meaningful work that this heaviness descended. This is a classic manifestation of the third hindrance-not a lack of interest or commitment, but a specific mental state that arises in relation to certain activities, often those that matter most to us.

Restlessness, the fourth hindrance, is perhaps the most normalized in our society. James, a senior executive, prided himself on his ability to handle multiple projects simultaneously. He was constantly busy, moving from meeting to meeting, responding to emails while on conference calls, and filling every moment with activity.

It wasn't until he began tracking his results that James realized his perpetual motion wasn't translating to meaningful outcomes. "I'm busy all day, but at the end of the week, I can't point to anything significant I've accomplished," he confessed. His restless mind, always jumping to the next task before completing the current one, was preventing him from bringing his full attention to any single priority.

Finally, skeptical doubt manifests as the voice that questions whether we're on the right path, whether we have what it takes, or whether our efforts will bear fruit. Lisa, a talented artist, spent years taking classes and workshops, always feeling that she needed "just one more" before she would be ready to show her work publicly.

"I keep thinking that the next teacher will give me the missing piece, the technique or insight that will finally make me feel confident," she explained. "But each class just leads to more questions and more doubt about whether I'm good enough."

Lisa's experience illustrates how doubt can keep us perpetually preparing but never actually doing-always seeking more information, more validation, more certainty before we're willing to commit to action.

The Relationship Between Hindrances and Suffering

What all these examples share is a common pattern: the hindrances arise, they divert us from our chosen path, and suffering results. This suffering takes many forms-the frustration of unrealized goals, the anxiety of constant busyness without meaningful progress, the self-criticism that comes from procrastination, or the quiet despair of watching our dreams remain perpetually out of reach.

Master Shi Heng Yi teaches that these hindrances place "dark clouds" on our minds or on the way of our climb. The metaphor is apt-just as clouds block the sun, these mental states obscure our clarity, our purpose, and our natural capacity for wise action.

The relationship between hindrances and suffering is not just psychological but practical. When we are caught in sensual desire, we sacrifice long-term fulfillment for momentary pleasure. When aversion drives our choices, we avoid the very experiences that would help us grow. Dullness prevents us from engaging fully with life, restlessness robs us of depth and presence, and doubt keeps us trapped in indecision and inaction.

Perhaps most significantly, these hindrances create a disconnect between our stated values and our lived experience. We say we want health, but sensual desire pulls us toward unhealthy foods. We claim to value growth, but aversion keeps us from embracing challenges. We aspire to meaningful work, but dullness, restlessness, or doubt prevent us from engaging fully with our chosen path.

This gap between intention and action is itself a source of suffering-the dissonance of knowing what matters to us yet finding ourselves unable to align our daily choices with those deeper values.

Recognizing Your Own Patterns

The path to working skillfully with the hindrances begins with recognition-the ability to see clearly when they are present and how they are operating in your life. This recognition is not about self-judgment or criticism, but about developing the capacity for honest self-observation.

Start by reflecting on your most important goals or aspirations-the "mountains" you are climbing in your life. Then consider: What consistently prevents you from making progress toward these goals? When you find yourself off track, what mental state typically precedes that diversion?

For some, the primary challenge is sensual desire-the pull toward immediate gratification that diverts energy from longer-term aspirations. For others, it's aversion-the tendency to avoid necessary discomfort or challenge. Still others might struggle primarily with dullness, restlessness, or doubt.

Most of us contend with all five hindrances at different times, but we often have one or two that arise most frequently or powerfully in our lives. Identifying these primary hindrances can focus our efforts and help us develop specific strategies for working with them.

Beyond recognizing which hindrances tend to arise for you, it's valuable to notice the patterns of when and how they appear. Are there specific triggers-certain types of tasks, particular times of day, specific environments or people-that tend to activate these mental states? Are there physical sensations, emotions, or thoughts that reliably precede the arising of a hindrance?

For instance, you might notice that sensual desire arises most strongly when you're tired or stressed, manifesting as the urge to check social media or eat comfort foods. Or you might observe that doubt tends to surface when you're working alone, without the external validation or feedback of others.

These patterns are not random. They reflect the specific conditions that tend to give rise to particular mental states for you. By recognizing these patterns, you gain valuable insight into how the hindrances operate in your life and where you might intervene most effectively.

It's also worth examining the stories or beliefs that accompany your hindrances. When sensual desire arises, what do you tell yourself to justify following it? When aversion appears, what reasons do you give for avoiding the discomfort? These narratives often reveal deeper beliefs about what you deserve, what you're capable of, or what's possible for you.

For example, the pull of sensual desire might be accompanied by thoughts like "I've been working hard, I deserve a break" or "Just five minutes won't hurt." Aversion might come with stories like "I need to be in the right mood to do this effectively" or "This is too difficult for me right now."

Recognizing these patterns-the specific hindrances that tend to arise for you, the conditions that trigger them, and the stories that sustain them-is not about self-criticism. It's about developing the clear seeing that is the foundation for any meaningful change.

As Master Shi Heng Yi teaches, the first step in the RAIN method for working with hindrances is precisely this recognition: seeing clearly what mental state is present. Without this recognition, we remain caught in unconscious patterns, wondering why we keep ending up in the same place despite our best intentions.

In the next chapter, we'll explore why this awareness is so essential and how to cultivate it more deeply in your life. For now, simply begin to notice: Which hindrances arise most frequently for you? Under what conditions do they appear? And what stories do you tell yourself when they're present? This honest self-observation, undertaken with curiosity rather than judgment, is the beginning of freedom from these obstacles to your path.

Notes

6

The Role of Awareness

In my early days of studying with Master Shi Heng Yi, I was eager to develop greater discipline in my life. Like many Westerners approaching Eastern wisdom traditions, I was drawn to the visible manifestations of self-mastery-the focus, the commitment, the unwavering dedication I observed in the Shaolin monks. I wanted to know: How could I develop that same level of discipline?

Master Shi Heng Yi's response surprised me. "Before discipline," he said, "must come awareness. Without awareness, discipline is just another form of unconscious pattern."

This insight-that awareness precedes discipline-has proven to be one of the most transformative teachings in my journey with the five hindrances. In this chapter, we'll explore why awareness is the essential foundation for working with these mental obstacles, how to become more sensitive to triggers and emotional states, and the journey from living on autopilot to embracing conscious choice.

Why Awareness Precedes Discipline

Many of us approach self-improvement with the belief that what we lack is willpower or discipline. We think, "If only I had more self-control, I could resist distractions" or "If I were more disciplined, I wouldn't procrastinate on important tasks." This perspective assumes that the solution to our challenges lies in forcing ourselves to behave differently through sheer determination.

Master Shi Heng Yi offers a different understanding. The issue is not primarily a lack of discipline but a lack of awareness. Without clear seeing, even the strongest willpower will be misdirected or ineffective.

Consider how the hindrances operate in your life. Sensual desire doesn't announce itself with a warning: "Attention! You are about to be diverted from your important work by the lure of social media." Instead, it arises subtly-perhaps as a slight feeling of restlessness or boredom, a momentary thought about checking your phone, and before you know it, you're scrolling through updates, having never made a conscious decision to abandon your original intention.

Similarly, aversion doesn't present itself clearly as "You are now avoiding this task because it feels uncomfortable." It disguises itself as reasonable-sounding excuses: "I'll be more effective if I wait until I'm in the right mood" or "I should organize my desk first so I can focus better."

Without awareness of these subtle processes-the arising of a hindrance, the accompanying physical sensations, the thoughts that justify following it-no amount of discipline will keep us on track. We'll continue to find ourselves diverted from our path without understanding why or how it happened.

This is why Master Shi Heng Yi emphasizes that awareness must come first. Only when we can see clearly what's happening in our minds can we make conscious choices about how to respond. Discipline without awareness is like trying to navigate a ship without knowing your position or destination-you might move with great force, but not necessarily in a useful direction.

The good news is that awareness can be cultivated. It's not a fixed trait but a skill that develops through practice. And as awareness grows, discipline naturally follows-not as a forced effort of will, but as the natural expression of clear seeing and conscious choice.

Becoming Sensitive to Triggers and Emotional States

How do we develop this essential awareness? Master Shi Heng Yi teaches that it begins with becoming more sensitive to what's happening within us and around us-particularly the triggers that tend to activate hindrances and the emotional states that accompany them.

This sensitivity is both physical and mental. On the physical level, it involves becoming more attuned to bodily sensations-the subtle tensions, energies, and feelings that signal the arising of a particular mental state. On the mental level, it means developing the capacity to observe thoughts and emotions without immediately identifying with them or being carried away by them.

I recall working with a client, Robert, who struggled with restlessness during important strategy sessions. Despite genuinely wanting to contribute meaningfully, he would find himself fidgeting, interrupting, or mentally checking out during these meetings. Through our work together, Robert began to notice that his restlessness was preceded by specific physical sensations-a tightness in his chest, a slight increase in his breathing rate, a feeling of heat rising in his body.

By becoming aware of these physical cues, Robert could recognize restlessness arising before it took over. This awareness created a crucial space between stimulus and response-a moment in which he could choose how to relate to the restlessness rather than being unconsciously driven by it.

Similarly, becoming sensitive to emotional triggers is essential for working with the hindrances. These triggers might be external-certain environments, people, or situations that tend to activate particular mental states-or internal, such as specific thoughts, memories, or emotional patterns.

For instance, you might notice that doubt tends to arise when you're comparing yourself to others, or that sensual desire becomes particularly strong when you're feeling stressed or depleted. Aversion might be triggered by tasks that feel ambiguous or open-ended, while dullness might arise when you're facing work that doesn't connect clearly to your deeper values.

Master Shi Heng Yi describes this sensitivity as a form of "reading"-the ability to feel into the structure and energy of a situation, just as he "reads" the density and structure of a brick before breaking it. This reading isn't intellectual analysis but a direct, embodied knowing that comes from paying close attention to your experience.

Developing this sensitivity requires practice. One approach is to pause several times throughout your day to check in with yourself: What physical sensations are present right now? What emotional tone colors your experience? What thoughts are moving through your mind? This simple practice of regular self-observation gradually builds the capacity to recognize patterns and triggers as they arise.

Another powerful practice is to reflect at the end of each day on moments when you were diverted from your intentions. Rather than judging these diversions, approach them with curiosity: What hindrance was operating? What triggered it? How did it feel in your body? What thoughts or stories accompanied it? This reflection builds awareness that will serve you in future similar situations.

The Journey from Autopilot to Conscious Living

Most of us spend much of our lives on autopilot-moving through our days based on habitual patterns, unconscious reactions, and unexamined assumptions. We respond to situations not based on clear seeing of what's actually happening, but on conditioned patterns established through past experiences.

This autopilot mode is what allows hindrances to operate so effectively. When we're not fully present and aware, these mental states can arise and take over without our noticing, leading us away from our chosen path before we even realize what's happening.

The journey from autopilot to conscious living is at the heart of Master Shi Heng Yi's teachings. It's a path of gradually awakening from the trance of habitual patterns and developing the capacity to live from awareness and choice rather than reaction and conditioning.

This journey isn't about achieving some perfect state of constant awareness-that's neither possible nor necessary. Rather, it's about developing the capacity to notice more quickly when you've gone on autopilot and to return to awareness more readily when you do.

I experienced this shift in my own relationship with the hindrance of doubt. For years, I would find myself caught in spirals of questioning and second-guessing important decisions, often without realizing it was happening. I would simply find myself stuck, unable to move forward, convinced that I needed more information or clarity before I could act.

As I developed greater awareness, I began to recognize the specific feeling of doubt arising-a particular constriction in my chest, a mental spinning quality, a subtle anxiety. This recognition allowed me to name what was happening: "Ah, this is doubt, the fifth hindrance." Simply naming it created a degree of freedom-I could see that this was a mental state arising, not an accurate reflection of reality or a command I had

51

to follow.

Over time, this awareness has deepened. Now I can often catch doubt as it first begins to arise, before it fully takes hold. This doesn't mean doubt no longer appears-it does-but my relationship to it has fundamentally changed. Instead of being unconsciously driven by it, I can recognize it, acknowledge it, and choose how to respond.

This is the essence of the journey from autopilot to conscious living-not the elimination of hindrances, but the development of a new relationship with them based on awareness and choice rather than unconscious reactivity.

Master Shi Heng Yi teaches that this journey unfolds gradually, through consistent practice and patient attention. It's not about dramatic breakthroughs but about the steady cultivation of awareness in daily life. Each time you notice a hindrance arising and choose to respond differently, you strengthen the muscle of conscious living.

The practices for developing this awareness need not be complex or time-consuming. Simple habits like pausing before beginning an important task to check in with your mental state, taking a few conscious breaths when you notice tension or reactivity arising, or setting regular reminders to step out of autopilot and return to presence-these small interventions can gradually transform your relationship with the hindrances.

As awareness grows, you'll likely notice that the hindrances don't disappear, but they begin to lose their power to divert you from your path. You'll catch them earlier, see them more clearly, and respond to them more skillfully. This is the foundation of true self-mastery-not the forceful control of experience through willpower, but the wise navigation of life through clear seeing and conscious choice.

In the next part of this book, we'll explore specific tools and practices for working with the hindrances once you've recognized them. But remember: without the foundation of awareness we've explored in this chapter, even the most powerful techniques will have limited effect. Awareness is the soil in which all other aspects of self-mastery take root and flourish.

Notes

Day:
Date & Month:

III

Tools and Practices for Transformation

Gain practical methods like the RAIN technique to overcome mental obstacles. Develop awareness, break old patterns, and build empowering habits through daily routines, mindful movement, and consistent self-inquiry

.

7

The RAIN Method-A Practical Path

Understanding the five hindrances is one thing; working with them effectively is quite another. Throughout my years of practice-both in monasteries and boardrooms-I've witnessed countless individuals grasp the concept of these mental obstacles intellectually, yet still find themselves repeatedly derailed by them in daily life.

This is where Master Shi Heng Yi's teaching of the RAIN method becomes invaluable. When I first encountered this approach during a retreat at the Shaolin Temple Europe, I was struck by its elegant simplicity and profound effectiveness. Here was a practical tool that could be applied in any situation, from high-stakes business negotiations to personal relationship challenges to moments of inner struggle.

The RAIN method consists of four steps: Recognize, Accept, Investigate, and Non-identification. Master Shi Heng Yi explains that this approach creates space between our awareness and our experience, allowing us to respond consciously rather than react habitually. Let's explore each step in detail.

Recognize: Identifying Your Current Mental State

The first step in the RAIN method is recognition-clearly seeing what mental state is present in this moment. As Master Shi Heng Yi teaches, "Along your journey, every day just sitting somewhere contemplating, learn to realize in which mental state are you actually finding yourself right now."

This recognition requires a quality of honest self-observation that many of us rarely practice. We're often so identified with our thoughts and emotions that we don't see them as mental states but as reality itself. When anger arises, we don't think, "I'm experiencing anger"; we simply feel angry and act from that place. When doubt clouds our mind, we don't recognize it as the fifth hindrance; we simply believe our doubts are valid concerns.

Recognition begins with pausing-creating a brief space between stimulus and response. In this pause, we can ask ourselves: What is happening in my mind right now? Which of the five hindrances, if any, might be present? Am I being pulled by sensual desire toward distraction? Am I pushing away discomfort through aversion? Am I caught in dullness, restlessness, or doubt?

I recall working with a senior executive who would become visibly agitated during certain meetings. Through our work together, he learned to recognize the specific sensation of heat rising in his chest that signaled restlessness was taking hold. This simple recognition-"Ah, restlessness is arising"-created a crucial moment of choice rather than automatic reaction.

Recognition doesn't require elaborate analysis or judgment. It's simply the clear seeing of what is. Master Shi Heng Yi compares it to reading the structure of a brick before breaking it-a direct, embodied knowing rather than intellectual understanding.

To develop this capacity for recognition, you might try a simple daily practice: Set a gentle reminder on your phone to pause several times throughout the day. When the reminder sounds, take a moment to check in with yourself. What mental state is present right now? Is there a hindrance at work? This regular check-in gradually builds the habit of recognition.

Accept: Embracing What Is, Without Judgment

The second step of the RAIN method is acceptance. This doesn't mean passive resignation or approval of negative states, but rather a willingness to acknowledge what is already happening without resistance.

Master Shi Heng Yi points out that the second hindrance-ill will or aversion-often arises in response to our own mental states. We feel restless, and then we become frustrated with our restlessness. We notice doubt arising, and then we criticize ourselves for being doubtful. This creates a secondary layer of suffering on top of the original hindrance.

Acceptance cuts through this cycle. It says simply, "Yes, this is what's happening right now." If you're experiencing doubt about an important decision, acceptance acknowledges, "Doubt is present." If you're feeling dull and unmotivated, acceptance notes, "Dullness is here."

This acceptance has a quality of kindness to it. Rather than judging ourselves for experiencing hindrances-which are, after all, universal human experiences-we meet these states with compassion and under-standing.

I've found that physically acknowledging acceptance can be helpful. When working with clients, I often suggest a simple gesture: placing a hand on the heart while silently saying, "This too is part of the human experience." This physical connection with oneself reinforces the attitude of kind acceptance.

One participant in a corporate workshop I led shared a powerful insight: "I've spent years fighting against my anxiety, which only made it worse. When I finally learned to accept its presence-not forever, but in this moment-something shifted. The anxiety didn't disappear, but my relationship to it changed completely."

This acceptance doesn't mean we abandon our goals or values. If we recognize that sensual desire is pulling us away from important work, we don't simply accept that we'll never complete the project. Rather, we accept that in this moment, the hindrance is present-and this very acceptance creates the conditions for wise action.

Investigate: Exploring the Roots and Triggers

With recognition and acceptance established, we can move to the third step: investigation. Here, we bring curious attention to the experience, exploring how this hindrance arose and what might be sustaining it.

Master Shi Heng Yi describes this investigation as detective work: "What is it like, how did I get into this state? Have I been in that state this morning already? No? So what happened since the morning until now that put me in this state?"

This investigation isn't abstract analysis but direct exploration of your experience. You might notice physical sensations associated with the hindrance-perhaps tension in the shoulders with restlessness, or heaviness in the limbs with dullness. You might observe the thoughts that accompany the state-the stories, judgments, or beliefs that fuel it.

Pay particular attention to triggers-the circumstances, interactions, or internal states that tend to activate specific hindrances. Perhaps sensual desire arises most strongly when you're tired or stressed. Maybe doubt surfaces primarily when you're working alone, without external validation.

A client of mine, a writer struggling with procrastination, discovered through investigation that her aversion to working on her book was triggered specifically by the moment of opening her document. Once she began writing, the aversion often dissolved, but that initial threshold was where the hindrance arose most powerfully. This precise understanding allowed her to develop targeted strategies for that specific trigger point.

Investigation also explores the consequences of following the hindrance. If you were to pursue that distraction, avoid that discomfort, or give in to that doubt, what would likely result? How might this affect your deeper goals and values?

Throughout this investigation, maintain the quality of acceptance established in the previous step. You're not investigating to criticize yourself but to understand with clarity and compassion how these patterns operate in your life.

Non-identification: Letting Go of Limiting Stories

The final step of the RAIN method is perhaps the most profound: non-identification. Master Shi Heng Yi describes this as learning not to identify too strongly with your body, mind, or emotional states.

This doesn't mean dissociating from your experience or denying your humanity. Rather, it's recognizing that you are not defined by or limited to any particular thought, emotion, or sensation. These experiences move through awareness like clouds through the sky, but they are not the sky itself.

When we over-identify with a hindrance-"I am an anxious person" rather than "Anxiety is present right now"-we become trapped in limiting stories about who we are and what's possible for us. Non-identification creates freedom from these constraints.

I often use the metaphor of a movie screen with my clients. The screen itself remains unchanged regardless of what film is projected onto it. In the same way, your essential awareness remains untouched by the various mental states that arise and pass within it.

This perspective shift is particularly powerful when working with persistent hindrances. A senior manager I coached had struggled with self-doubt throughout her career, constantly questioning her decisions and abilities despite consistent success. Through practicing non-identification, she began to recognize doubt as "weather" passing through her awareness rather than a fixed aspect of her identity. "I'm not a doubtful person," she realized. "I'm a person who sometimes experiences doubt, just like everyone else."

Non-identification allows us to hold our experience more lightly. We can acknowledge the presence of a hindrance without being defined or controlled by it. This creates space for wise response rather than automatic reaction.

The RAIN method isn't a one-time solution but a practice to be applied repeatedly. Each time you work through these four steps-Recognize, Accept, Investigate, Non-identify-you strengthen your capacity to relate skillfully to hindrances rather than being unconsciously driven by them.

As Master Shi Heng Yi teaches, the goal isn't to eliminate hindrances entirely-they are part of the human experience-but to develop a new relationship with them based on awareness and choice rather than identification and reactivity.

In my own life, the RAIN method has transformed how I relate to challenging mental states. What once seemed like insurmountable obstacles now appear as passing weather patterns in the wider sky of awareness. This doesn't mean the hindrances no longer arise-they do-but their power to derail me has diminished significantly through this practice of mindful engagement.

Notes

Day:
Date & Month:

8

Breaking Patterns and Building New Habits

We are, to a remarkable degree, creatures of habit. Research suggests that up to 45% of our daily actions are not conscious choices but habitual patterns operating below the level of awareness. These patterns-in how we think, feel, and behave-shape our lives more profoundly than we typically realize.

Master Shi Heng Yi addresses this reality directly: "So many of us live in the same cycles of unhappiness and suffering. I witnessed it in my life as well because I felt I was never enough." He describes how patterns established in childhood-the pressure to achieve, the sense of never being sufficient-created emotional walls and shaped his responses to life for decades.

Breaking free from limiting patterns and establishing new, empowering habits is essential for self-mastery. In this chapter, we'll explore practical approaches to identifying and replacing old patterns, the power of consistency in creating lasting change, and how to design a personal training regimen that integrates mind and body.

How to Identify and Replace Old Patterns

The first step in changing any pattern is becoming aware of its existence. As Master Shi Heng Yi states simply, "Number one, you need to see you have one." This awareness often begins with recognizing recurring outcomes in your life. Do you consistently find yourself in similar relationship dynamics? Do you repeatedly start projects with enthusiasm only to abandon them? Do certain emotional reactions arise predictably in specific situations?

These recurring outcomes point to underlying patterns that may operate largely outside your conscious awareness. To identify these patterns more clearly, try this reflective exercise: Choose an area of your life where you feel stuck or dissatisfied. Then ask yourself:

- What specific outcome keeps recurring in this area?
- What actions or behaviors typically precede this outcome?
- What thoughts, emotions, or beliefs are present during these behaviors?
- When did this pattern first develop in my life?
- What function might this pattern have served originally?

I've guided hundreds of individuals through this process, and the insights can be remarkable. One client, a talented artist who repeatedly sabotaged opportunities for recognition, traced this pattern to a childhood experience where standing out led to painful social rejection. The pattern of self-sabotage had originally served as protection-a function that was no longer necessary but still operating automatically.

Once you've identified a pattern, the next step is to consciously design its replacement. Master Shi Heng Yi is clear: "Number two, you need to replace old patterns." This replacement isn't just about stopping the old behavior but about establishing a new, more beneficial one in its place.

Effective replacement patterns share several characteristics:

1. They address the same underlying need or trigger as the original pattern
2. They align with your deeper values and goals
3. They're specific and actionable
4. They're realistic given your current resources and circumstances

For example, if you identify a pattern of seeking distraction through social media whenever you feel anxious about a challenging task, your replacement pattern might be: "When I notice anxiety about a task, I'll take three conscious breaths, acknowledge the feeling, and then work for just five minutes before reassessing."

This replacement addresses the same trigger (anxiety), aligns with your values (completing meaningful work), provides a specific action (breathe, acknowledge, work for five minutes), and remains realistic (a small, manageable step rather than an overwhelming commitment).

The Power of Consistency and Daily Training

Identifying a replacement pattern is only the beginning. Establishing it as a new habit requires consistent practice over time. Master Shi Heng Yi emphasizes this point strongly: "It's not helpful to like six days per week do nothing and then you go one day to the gym and give your everything. No, it's better you have some type of consistency throughout the whole day. This is what builds patterns, healthy patterns."

This principle applies whether you're developing physical strength, emotional regulation, mental focus, or any other aspect of self-mastery. Consistency trumps intensity. A daily ten-minute meditation practice will transform your mind more effectively than a monthly three-hour retreat. Regular brief moments of conscious breathing throughout your day will build greater emotional regulation than occasional deep breathing sessions during crises.

I've found that the concept of "minimum viable commitment" helps establish consistency. Rather than setting ambitious targets that become unsustainable, identify the smallest version of a practice that you can commit to without fail. Can you meditate for two minutes daily? Can you do a single push-up each morning? Can you write one paragraph of your book before checking email?

These minimal commitments serve as anchors for consistency. Once established, they naturally tend to expand over time. The writer who consistently shows up for one paragraph often finds themselves writing for pages. The meditator who never misses their two-minute practice gradually extends to five, ten, or twenty minutes.

Another powerful approach is habit stacking-attaching a new habit to an established one. If you already make coffee every morning, use the time while the water boils for a brief standing meditation. If you already commute to work, use the first five minutes to practice conscious breathing or positive visualization.

The key insight about consistency is that it's not primarily about willpower but about designing your environment and routines to support your new patterns. Make the desired behavior the path of least resistance. Place your meditation cushion prominently in your living room. Keep healthy snacks at eye level in your refrigerator. Set your workout clothes out the night before. These environmental supports reduce the decision energy required for consistency.

Creating a Personal Training Regimen for Mind and Body

Master Shi Heng Yi's approach to self-mastery is holistic, integrating mind and body rather than treating them as separate domains. This integration is reflected in the Shaolin training regimen, which develops physical capabilities alongside mental qualities like focus, resilience, and awareness.

Drawing from this tradition, a comprehensive personal training regimen addresses multiple dimensions of development:

Physical Training: Regular movement that builds strength, flexibility, and endurance. This might include formal exercise, but also mindful walking, standing practices, or conscious engagement with daily physical tasks. The specific form matters less than the quality of presence you bring to it.

Mental Training: Practices that develop focus, clarity, and awareness. Meditation is the classic approach, but mental training can also include reading that challenges your thinking, engaging with complex problems, or simply practicing sustained attention on a single task without multitasking.

Emotional Training: Developing greater awareness of and skill with emotional states. This might include journaling about emotional patterns, practicing the RAIN method with difficult feelings, or consciously cultivating positive states like gratitude, compassion, or joy.

Relational Training: Practices that enhance your connection with others. This could involve deep listening exercises, conscious communication, acts of service, or intentional cultivation of empathy and understanding.

Spiritual Training: Connecting with something larger than yourself, whether through formal religious practice, time in nature, creative expression, or contemplation of life's deeper questions.

The most effective training regimen integrates these dimensions rather than compartmentalizing them. For example, a mindful walk in nature can simultaneously be physical training (movement), mental training (present-moment awareness), emotional training (processing feelings), and spiritual training (connection with the natural world).

Start by assessing your current patterns in each dimension. Where are you already strong? Where do you see opportunities for growth? Then design simple, sustainable practices that address your priorities while fitting realistically into your life.

Remember that a training regimen is not static but evolves with your development. As Master Shi Heng Yi's brick-breaking demonstration illustrates, mastery involves progressive challenges. In Shaolin training, practitioners begin with wooden materials before advancing to stone and eventually metal. Similarly, your personal regimen should include appropriate progression as your capabilities develop.

The ultimate aim of this training isn't perfection but integration—bringing your whole being into greater harmony and alignment. As you consistently practice your regimen, you'll likely notice that the boundaries between dimensions begin to blur. Physical training becomes mental training. Emotional regulation enhances relationships. Spiritual connection informs daily actions.

This integration reflects Master Shi Heng Yi's fundamental teaching: true self-mastery isn't about controlling or forcing your experience but about cultivating the awareness, discipline, and wisdom to live in alignment with your deeper nature and values.

By identifying and replacing limiting patterns, establishing consistency in your practice, and creating a holistic training regimen, you lay the foundation for lasting transformation. These approaches don't promise overnight results, but they offer something more valuable: sustainable growth that emerges naturally from daily choices and consistent practice.

Notes

Day:
Date & Month:

9

Mind-Body Unity-Focus, Energy, and Endurance

One of the most striking demonstrations of Master Shi Heng Yi's teachings is his ability to break bricks with his bare hand. When I first witnessed this feat during a retreat, I was initially impressed by what seemed like extraordinary physical strength. However, as Master Shi Heng Yi explained the process, I realized I was observing something far more profound: the perfect integration of mind and body working as a unified whole.

"The key to breaking this brick isn't strength necessarily," he explains. "It's the ability to really, really focus." This statement encapsulates a fundamental principle of self-mastery: the power of focused intention, the unity of mind and body, and the capacity to channel energy precisely where it's needed.

In this chapter, we'll explore how to develop this mind-body unity through understanding the metaphor of breaking bricks, practicing mindful movement and breathwork, and building willpower through integrated physical and mental training.

The Metaphor of Breaking Bricks: Focus Over Force

When Master Shi Heng Yi approaches a brick, he doesn't simply strike it with maximum force. Instead, he first "reads" the brick-feeling its structure, density, and unique properties. "When I touch the stone," he explains, "I literally feel inside the structure of the stone. I feel the density of the stone in my fingers... I know how the energy is going to come down."

This process of reading and responding is fundamentally different from imposing force. It's about understanding what's in front of you and aligning your energy with that reality rather than fighting against it. The brick breaks not because it's overwhelmed by superior force, but because energy is applied with perfect precision at exactly the right point.

This metaphor offers profound guidance for approaching life's challenges. Whether facing a difficult conversation, a creative block, a business problem, or an emotional struggle, the principle remains the same: focus trumps force. Understanding the structure of the situation-its unique properties, tensions, and potentials-allows for precisely directed energy rather than wasted effort.

I've applied this approach in my corporate consulting work with remarkable results. When teams face seemingly intractable problems, I guide them to "read" the situation deeply before attempting solutions. What are the underlying structures and dynamics? Where are the points of tension? Where might energy be most effectively applied? This focused approach often reveals elegant solutions that brute-force problem-solving would miss entirely.

The brick-breaking metaphor also illuminates the nature of obstacles. Just as the brick appears solid and impenetrable, our challenges often seem insurmountable when viewed as monolithic wholes. But everything has an internal structure with points of greater and lesser resistance. Finding these points-the fault lines in the brick-transforms what seems impossible into something achievable through focused intention.

To apply this metaphor in your own life, practice "reading" situations before responding to them:

- When facing a challenging task, take time to understand its structure before diving in
- In difficult conversations, listen deeply to grasp the underlying dynamics rather than reacting to surface tensions
- With personal obstacles, explore their composition-what elements are present, and how are they connected?
- Notice where you're applying force without focus, and experiment with more precisely directed energy

This practice of reading and responding develops what Master Shi Heng Yi calls "sensitivity"-the capacity to feel into the nature of things rather than imposing our preconceptions upon them.

Mindful Movement, Breathwork, and Standing Practice

The unity of mind and body isn't an abstract concept but a lived experience developed through specific practices. Master Shi Heng Yi emphasizes three fundamental approaches: mindful movement, conscious breathing, and standing practice.

Mindful Movement: Any physical activity can become a vehicle for developing mind-body unity when approached with full presence. The key is bringing complete attention to the experience-feeling the sensations, noticing the breath, observing the mind's response.

In the Shaolin tradition, martial arts forms serve as moving meditations that develop this integration. However, you don't need to practice kung fu to experience mindful movement. Walking, swimming, dancing, yoga, or even household chores can become powerful practices when infused with presence.

Try this simple exercise: Choose an everyday movement like walking or washing dishes. As you engage in the activity, bring your full attention to the physical sensations-the feeling of your feet touching the ground, the temperature of the water on your hands. When your mind wanders, gently return your attention to the sensations. This basic practice begins to bridge the habitual gap between mind and body.

Breathwork: The breath occupies a unique position as both voluntary and involuntary, conscious and unconscious. This makes it an ideal bridge between mind and body, a tool for influencing states that might otherwise seem beyond our control.

Master Shi Heng Yi's morning routine includes conscious breathing-deliberately regulating the breath to influence energy and awareness. This practice has both immediate and cumulative effects, calming the nervous system in the moment while gradually developing greater sensitivity to subtle energies.

A foundational breathwork practice is simply observing the natural breath without attempting to change it. Sit comfortably, close your eyes, and place your attention on the sensations of breathing. Notice the temperature of the air, the movement of your chest and abdomen, the subtle pause between inhalation and exhalation. When your attention wanders, gently return it to the breath.

As this practice becomes comfortable, you might explore more active breathing techniques, such as extending the exhalation (calming) or emphasizing the inhalation (energizing). The key is maintaining awareness throughout, noticing how different patterns affect your physical and mental state.

Standing Practice: Perhaps the most distinctive of Master Shi Heng

Yi's recommendations is standing practice-holding specific postures for extended periods to build both physical strength and mental willpower. "I choose one position that I'm standing in and then I hold that position for 15 minutes," he explains.

These practices might seem strange to Western sensibilities accustomed to movement-based exercise. However, standing practices have profound effects on both body and mind. Physically, they develop core strength, improve posture, and build endurance. Mentally, they cultivate willpower, presence, and the capacity to remain centered amid discomfort.

A simple standing practice is the "embracing the tree" posture from qigong: Stand with feet shoulder-width apart, knees slightly bent. Raise your arms as if embracing a large tree trunk, elbows lower than shoulders. Relax your shoulders while maintaining the position. Begin with just one minute and gradually extend the duration as your capacity increases.

The key insight about these practices is that they're not merely physical exercises but integrated training for the whole being. As Master Shi Heng Yi explains, "Willpower and development of energy go hand in hand with each other." By challenging yourself to remain present and focused during physical discomfort, you develop capacities that transfer to every area of life.

Building Willpower Through Physical and Mental Training

Willpower-the capacity to direct your energy consciously rather than being driven by immediate impulses-is essential for self-mastery. Yet many people approach willpower development backwards, attempting to force themselves through sheer determination rather than systematically building this capacity through appropriate training.

Master Shi Heng Yi offers a more effective approach: willpower, like any other quality, can be developed gradually through consistent practice. The standing postures described above are perfect examples-they create controlled challenges that stretch your capacity without overwhelming it.

This progressive approach applies to both physical and mental training. Just as you wouldn't attempt to lift 300 pounds without first building up to it, you shouldn't expect to maintain perfect focus for hours without developing that capacity incrementally.

Start with brief but consistent practices that challenge you slightly beyond your comfort zone. If you can maintain focused attention for three minutes, practice for four. If you can hold a standing posture for one minute, aim for ninety seconds. These small stretches, consistently applied, gradually expand your capacity.

The integration of physical and mental training accelerates this development. Physical practices like standing postures, mindful movement, or breathwork provide tangible feedback that helps calibrate your effort. You can feel when you're applying too much tension or not enough engagement. This bodily wisdom then transfers to mental challenges, where the feedback might otherwise be less clear.

I've found that alternating between physical and mental willpower challenges creates a powerful synergy. A client struggling with procrastination on a writing project established a routine of brief standing practice followed immediately by focused writing. The physical discipline created momentum that carried into the mental task, making it easier to overcome initial resistance.

This integrated approach also develops what Master Shi Heng Yi calls "reading"-the ability to sense and direct energy. Through physical practices, you learn to feel subtle energetic states in the body. This sensitivity then extends to emotional and mental energies, allowing for more skillful navigation of internal states.

The ultimate aim of this training isn't to eliminate discomfort but to develop a new relationship with it. Discomfort becomes information rather than an emergency-a sensation to be observed and worked with rather than automatically avoided.

A senior executive I coached described this shift eloquently after six months of integrated practice: "I used to think willpower meant gritting my teeth and forcing myself forward. Now I understand it's more like surfing-feeling the energy of the wave and moving with it skillfully rather than fighting against it."

This perspective aligns perfectly with Master Shi Heng Yi's brick-breaking demonstration. The brick doesn't break because he forces it to submit but because he understands its nature and applies energy with perfect precision. Similarly, self-mastery isn't about dominating yourself through force but about understanding your nature and working with it wisely.

The practices outlined in this chapter-focused attention, mindful movement, breathwork, standing postures, and progressive willpower training-develop this capacity for wise engagement with yourself and the world. They build not just strength or discipline in isolation, but the integrated quality of mind-body unity that characterizes true self-mastery.

As you incorporate these practices into your life, remember that their power lies not in perfection but in presence-the quality of awareness you bring to each moment of training. Even a brief standing practice done with complete attention will develop mind-body unity more effectively than longer sessions performed mechanically or distractedly.

Start where you are, with practices that challenge you appropriately without overwhelming your current capacity. Trust in the power of consistency over time. Just as Master Shi Heng Yi didn't develop his brick-breaking ability overnight but through years of dedicated practice, your own capacity for focus, energy, and endurance will develop gradually through patient, persistent training.

Notes

Day:
Date & Month:

IV

Building Character and Virtue

*Delve into the Shaolin virtues and their role in shaping
character. Learn how to cultivate discipline, patience, and
resilience, and why training virtues is as important as
physical or mental skills for true self-mastery.*

10

The Shaolin Virtues-Your Inner Framework

During my years of corporate leadership, I often observed a curious phe-
nomenon: two individuals with nearly identical skills and intelligence
would achieve drastically different outcomes. One would rise steadily,
earning trust and creating lasting impact, while the other would plateau
or even derail despite their talents. The difference, I discovered, wasn't
in their abilities but in their character-the internal framework that
guided their decisions and actions.

This observation led me to one of Master Shi Heng Yi's most
profound teachings: the 14 Shaolin virtues. As he explains, "When
a disciple comes to join this monastery, there are so-called 14 virtues
within the Shaolin Temple." These virtues aren't abstract philosophical
concepts but practical qualities that form the foundation of self-mastery
and meaningful achievement.

What struck me most about Master Shi Heng Yi's approach to these
virtues is how he organizes them: "Those 14 virtues, I try to make it
simple, are separated into virtues that we are expecting people to have

when they arrive here and the group of virtues that can be learned." This practical categorization acknowledges that character development is both about cultivating what we already possess and systematically developing new qualities.

The 14 Shaolin Virtues: Expected, Action, and Mind

The Shaolin virtues fall into three categories: expected virtues (those we should already possess to some degree), virtues of action (those that guide our external behavior), and virtues of mind (those that shape our internal landscape).

The expected virtues include:

Self-control: The ability to regulate your impulses, emotions, and behaviors. This isn't about suppression but about conscious choice-responding rather than reacting.

Discipline: Master Shi Heng Yi places special emphasis on this virtue, noting that it's one of the qualities expected before training even begins: "Amongst one of them is discipline, and the reason why is simply like this: I think the human is able to develop and learn so many different things when the willingness is there." Discipline transforms willingness into consistent action.

Benevolence: A genuine concern for the well-being of others and the desire to act in ways that benefit them.

Modesty: The ability to acknowledge your limitations and remain open to learning, regardless of your achievements or status.

The virtues of action include:

Loyalty: Steadfast commitment to people, principles, and purposes you've chosen to serve.

Trust: Both being trustworthy and extending appropriate trust to others.

Respect: Recognizing the inherent dignity and worth of all beings.

Righteousness: Aligning your actions with moral principles rather than mere convenience or self-interest.

Courage: The willingness to act despite fear, uncertainty, or discomfort.

The virtues of mind include:

Willpower: The mental strength to persist despite obstacles or distractions.

Perseverance: Continuing steadily on your chosen path despite difficulties or delays.

Persistence: Closely related to perseverance, this virtue emphasizes maintaining effort even when results aren't immediately visible.

Patience: The capacity to accept delay, difficulty, or discomfort without becoming agitated or giving up.

Endurance: The ability to withstand hardship or stress over extended periods.

These virtues aren't isolated qualities but an interconnected framework. Like the structure of a building, each virtue supports and reinforces the others. Discipline enables perseverance, self-control facilitates respect, courage makes righteousness possible, and so on. Together, they form what Master Shi Heng Yi calls "the framework of the character."

I've witnessed the power of this framework in my own journey from corporate leadership to monastic training and back to the world of coaching and teaching. When I faced the initial challenges of monastic life-the physical discomfort, the surrender of autonomy, the confrontation with my own ego-it was these virtues that carried me through. Later, when I returned to work with organizations and individuals, these same virtues provided a compass for navigating complex ethical dilemmas and leadership challenges.

Training Virtues Like Discipline, Patience, and Perseverance

The most revolutionary aspect of Master Shi Heng Yi's teaching on virtues is that they can be systematically developed-trained like muscles through consistent practice. This approach stands in stark contrast to the common Western belief that character is largely fixed or determined early in life.

Master Shi Heng Yi explains: "When you are willing to learn, you are willing to learn, and afterwards you put that willingness into a form. Willingness into a form means you make a plan, a simple daily plan." This practical approach transforms virtue from an abstract ideal into a concrete practice.

How do we train these virtues? The process parallels physical training in many ways:

Start where you are: Just as you wouldn't begin a fitness program with advanced exercises, virtue training begins with honest assessment of your current strengths and limitations. Perhaps you already possess strong discipline but struggle with patience, or maybe your courage is well-developed while self-control needs attention.

Progressive challenge: Effective training gradually increases the difficulty of the challenge. If you're developing patience, you might begin with practicing it in minor irritations before tackling major frustrations. For perseverance, start with completing smaller projects before taking on more demanding long-term commitments.

Consistent practice: Master Shi Heng Yi emphasizes that virtues develop through daily consistency rather than occasional heroic efforts. Small, regular actions build the neural pathways and habits that eventually become character.

Integrated approach: Virtues aren't developed in isolation but through real-life application across different domains. Patience practiced in traffic strengthens patience needed in difficult conversations. Discipline in maintaining a meditation practice reinforces discipline in professional commitments.

I've found that creating specific training opportunities for each virtue accelerates development. For discipline, establish a small daily practice (meditation, exercise, study) and maintain it without exception. For patience, deliberately place yourself in situations that typically trigger impatience, bringing awareness to your reactions. For perseverance, commit to completing projects that require sustained effort over time.

One executive I coached created what she called "virtue challenges"- weekly practices designed to strengthen specific qualities she wanted to develop. To build courage, she committed to one difficult conversation each week. For discipline, she established a morning routine that began 30 minutes earlier than her natural inclination. For patience, she chose the longest checkout line at the grocery store rather than the shortest.

These practices might seem trivial, but their cumulative effect is profound. As Master Shi Heng Yi teaches, "The small things matter. If you cannot handle the little things like writing down your goals on a piece of paper or keeping your living space clean, then you cannot handle the big things."

The ultimate aim of virtue training isn't moral perfection but the development of an inner framework strong enough to support your deepest aspirations and withstand life's inevitable challenges. When this framework is solid, external achievements flow more naturally and sustainably. Without it, even the most impressive accomplishments remain fragile, vulnerable to collapse under pressure.

As we move into the next chapter, we'll explore how these virtues manifest in daily life and relationships, transforming abstract qualities into lived reality. The journey of character development is lifelong, but each step builds upon the last, gradually revealing the person you're capable of becoming.

Notes

Day:
Date & Month:

11

Virtue in Action-Living with Integrity

Understanding the Shaolin virtues conceptually is one thing; embodying them in daily life is quite another. During my time at the monastery, I observed how Master Shi Heng Yi and the other monks didn't merely discuss virtues-they lived them through every action, from the most mundane tasks to the most challenging situations. This integration of virtue into action is what Master Shi Heng Yi calls "living with integrity"-a wholeness where inner values and outer behavior align seamlessly.

In my subsequent work with leaders and organizations, I've seen how this alignment creates not just personal fulfillment but also sustainable success and positive impact. When virtues remain theoretical, they provide little benefit. It's only when they're expressed through concrete actions and relationships that their transformative power becomes evident.

Applying Virtues in Daily Life and Relationships

The application of virtues begins with awareness-recognizing opportunities to express these qualities in everyday situations. These opportunities aren't limited to dramatic moments of crisis or decision but are present in the fabric of ordinary life.

Consider how virtues might manifest in common scenarios:

In professional settings, self-control appears as maintaining composure during tense meetings or disagreements. Discipline shows up as consistent follow-through on commitments. Respect manifests as giving full attention to colleagues and direct reports, while courage might mean speaking an unpopular truth when necessary.

In personal relationships, patience reveals itself in listening fully before responding to a partner's concerns. Benevolence appears as small acts of kindness without expectation of return. Trust shows up as vulnerability and openness, while loyalty means standing by loved ones through difficulties.

In relation to yourself, modesty enables honest self-assessment without defensive justification. Perseverance means continuing healthy practices even when motivation wanes. Righteousness guides choices toward what serves your deeper values rather than momentary impulses.

Master Shi Heng Yi emphasizes that virtues must be practiced consistently rather than selectively. It's relatively easy to display patience with those we admire or in situations where we're comfortable. The true test comes when dealing with difficult people or challenging circumstances. Can you maintain respect when someone has disrespected you? Can you practice benevolence toward those who show none in return?

This consistent application doesn't mean rigid adherence to rules but rather a fluid expression of principles adapted to context. As Master Shi Heng Yi notes, "It is not very useful or wise to tell the truth at the wrong times. If someone is hungry, they do not want principles, they only want the bread to eat." This wisdom recognizes that virtues must be applied with sensitivity to circumstances and needs.

I've found that creating specific intentions for virtue expression helps bridge the gap between concept and action. Before entering a meeting, you might set an intention to practice patience and respect regardless of how others behave. Before a family gathering, you might commit to benevolence and self-control even if tensions arise. These conscious intentions gradually become habitual responses.

Relationships provide particularly fertile ground for virtue development. The friction of human interaction inevitably triggers our reactive patterns, creating perfect opportunities to practice self-control, patience, and benevolence. Rather than avoiding difficult relationships, we can approach them as training grounds for character development.

A senior executive I worked with transformed her relationship with a challenging board member by reframing their interactions as opportunities to develop patience and self-control. What had been a source of dread became a valuable practice arena. Not only did her stress decrease, but the relationship itself gradually improved as her responses changed.

The Role of Character in Handling Power and Success

Perhaps nowhere is the importance of virtue more evident than in how we handle power and success. History and contemporary life are filled with examples of talented individuals who achieved positions of influence only to be undone by character flaws that went unaddressed.

Master Shi Heng Yi teaches that power amplifies whatever qualities are already present. If your framework of virtues is strong, power becomes a tool for positive impact. If that framework is weak or imbalanced, power often corrupts or destroys. This is why the Shaolin tradition places character development before the teaching of powerful techniques.

Success presents similar challenges. Without a strong virtue framework, achievements often lead to arrogance, attachment, or insatiable craving for more. With that framework in place, success can be appreciated without becoming a source of identity or addiction.

I witnessed this principle during my corporate career, where I saw brilliant leaders fail not because of strategic errors but because of character deficiencies-inability to control impulses, lack of respect for others, impatience with necessary processes, or courage that deteriorated into recklessness. Conversely, the most effective and respected leaders I encountered weren't necessarily the most naturally talented but those who had developed the strongest character foundations.

Master Shi Heng Yi describes this quality as being "unshakable," which he defines as "being at peace with yourself. More specifically, there is nothing anyone can add nor subtract from you. You are not inflated by compliments nor are you torn down by criticism. When you enter a room, you know what to do, and others can sense this."

This unshakability comes from the integration of virtues into a coherent whole-what we might call integrity. The word "integrity" shares its root with "integer," meaning whole or complete. When virtues are fully integrated into your being, there's no gap between who you are and how you act, between what you believe and what you do.

Developing this integrity requires honest self-reflection. Where do gaps exist between your stated values and your actual behavior? In what situations do you find your virtues most challenged? What patterns of compromise have become habitual? These questions aren't meant to induce guilt but to identify opportunities for growth and integration.

A practice I recommend to clients is the evening review-a few minutes at day's end to reflect on how you expressed or failed to express your core virtues. This isn't about harsh self-judgment but about learning and recommitment. Where did you successfully embody patience, courage, or benevolence? Where did you fall short? What might you do differently tomorrow?

Over time, this practice creates greater congruence between values and actions. The gaps narrow. Integrity strengthens. Character becomes not just an aspiration but a lived reality expressed through daily choices and relationships.

As Master Shi Heng Yi teaches, "The purpose is not to teach Shaolin arts to learn to fight, but to find different ways of investigating yourself and investigating things around you." This investigation reveals both our current limitations and our potential for growth-a potential that becomes realized through the consistent application of virtues in every aspect of life.

Notes

Day:
Date & Month:

12

Resilience and Growth-Embracing Discomfort

One of the most powerful moments in my training with Master Shi Heng Yi came during a particularly challenging standing practice. As my legs burned and my mind screamed for relief, he approached quietly and said, "Everything that you feel is difficult for you, find a way to still do it. As long as you can do the things, stop listening to the mind."

This simple instruction contains a profound truth about resilience and growth: our capacity expands only when we move beyond comfort into challenge. In the Shaolin tradition, this principle isn't just philosophical-it's embedded in every aspect of training, from physical postures to mental disciplines to spiritual practices.

Modern life often encourages us to avoid discomfort at all costs. Convenience, comfort, and immediate gratification are marketed as ideals. Yet as Master Shi Heng Yi teaches, this pursuit of constant comfort actually diminishes us, narrowing our capabilities and reducing our resilience. True growth-in strength, wisdom, or character-requires embracing rather than avoiding difficulty.

The Necessity of Doing Hard Things

The path of least resistance rarely leads to meaningful development. This truth applies across all domains of human experience:

Physical growth requires challenging muscles beyond their current capacity. Mental growth demands grappling with complex ideas rather than simplistic explanations. Emotional growth comes from facing difficult feelings rather than numbing or avoiding them. Spiritual growth emerges from questioning comfortable assumptions and confronting existential realities.

Master Shi Heng Yi expresses this principle through his teaching on opposites: "We must examine opposite ends of the spectrum when we seek balance. If we desire comfort we must also know discomfort. If we seek relaxation then we must also understand stress. Knowing both sides draws a complete map with which we can navigate towards balance more capably."

This willingness to engage with difficulty doesn't mean seeking suffering for its own sake. Rather, it means recognizing that challenges are not obstacles to a good life but essential components of one. They are the resistance against which we develop strength, the questions that deepen our understanding, the obstacles that reveal our capabilities.

I've observed this principle at work in countless contexts. Athletes who avoid painful training plateaued in their development. Executives who sidestepped difficult conversations saw their influence diminish. Relationships that avoided necessary conflicts eventually lost depth and authenticity. In each case, the avoidance of discomfort led not to happiness but to stagnation.

Conversely, those who willingly embraced difficulty-not recklessly but intentionally-discovered capacities they didn't know they possessed. The runner who pushed through the wall of fatigue, the leader who initiated the conversation everyone else avoided, the couple who worked through painful differences rather than papering over them-all emerged stronger and more capable than before.

This willingness to do hard things isn't about masochism or proving toughness. It's about recognizing that our comfort zones, while necessary for rest and integration, become prisons when we never venture beyond them. As Master Shi Heng Yi teaches, "Directly approaching what you want is the wrong way. If you want freedom, for example, you must explore structure and discipline. If you can find freedom within the discipline then you have found true freedom."

Expanding Your Comfort Zone, Step by Step

While embracing discomfort is necessary for growth, how we approach this process matters greatly. Master Shi Heng Yi doesn't advocate throwing yourself into overwhelming challenges but rather expanding your comfort zone gradually through consistent practice.

This progressive approach follows several principles:

Start with manageable challenges-difficult enough to stimulate growth but not so difficult that they overwhelm your current capacity. If you've never run, begin with alternating walking and jogging rather than attempting a marathon. If public speaking terrifies you, practice with a small supportive group before addressing a large audience.

Focus on process rather than outcome. The goal isn't the achievement itself but the development that comes through engagement with challenge. A beginning meditator who sits for five minutes with full presence has succeeded, regardless of whether their mind was perfectly calm.

Build consistency before intensity. Regular engagement with moderate challenges produces more sustainable growth than occasional heroic efforts followed by exhaustion or injury. The Shaolin approach emphasizes daily practice over sporadic extreme exertion.

Recognize the rhythm of challenge and recovery. Growth doesn't occur during the challenge itself but during the recovery period that follows. Constant strain without adequate rest leads not to growth but to breakdown. The skilled practitioner learns to balance pushing limits with allowing integration.

I've found that creating a deliberate practice of discomfort accelerates growth across all domains. This might involve physical challenges like cold showers or fasting, social challenges like initiating conversations with strangers, or mental challenges like studying complex subjects outside your expertise. The specific form matters less than the consistent willingness to step beyond comfort.

One client, a successful but risk-averse professional, created what she called a "discomfort curriculum"-a progressive series of challenges designed to expand her comfort zone across different areas of life. She began with small steps: ordering a meal she'd never tried, taking a different route to work, expressing an unpopular opinion in a low-stakes setting. As her comfort zone expanded, so did her challenges: solo travel to unfamiliar places, public speaking engagements, difficult but necessary conversations with family members.

The transformation was remarkable. Not only did she develop specific skills and confidences, but her entire relationship to difficulty changed. What had once seemed threatening now appeared as opportunity. Her resilience-the capacity to respond effectively to challenges rather than being diminished by them-increased dramatically.

Learning from Adversity and Uncertainty

While intentional challenges build capacity, life inevitably presents unplanned difficulties as well. Job loss, relationship endings, health crises, financial setbacks-these experiences can't be scheduled or controlled. Yet they too can become sources of growth rather than merely suffering to be endured.

Master Shi Heng Yi teaches that our response to adversity reveals and shapes our character more profoundly than our response to success. Anyone can display virtue when things are going well. The true test comes when we face loss, disappointment, or uncertainty.

This perspective transforms how we view life's difficulties. Rather than asking, "Why is this happening to me?" we can ask, "What might this teach me? How might this strengthen me? What qualities am I being called to develop through this experience?"

I've witnessed this transformative reframing countless times in my work with individuals facing major life transitions. A corporate executive who lost his position after twenty years initially experienced only shame and disorientation. As he shifted his perspective, he began to see the layoff as an opportunity to rediscover values and capacities that had been submerged in his single-minded career focus. What began as catastrophe became-though not without real pain and struggle-a catalyst for authentic growth.

Uncertainty presents particular challenges for many of us. We crave certainty, predictability, and control, yet life consistently refuses to provide these completely. The COVID-19 pandemic offered a global lesson in this reality, as carefully constructed plans and assumptions collapsed virtually overnight.

Master Shi Heng Yi's teaching on uncertainty emphasizes presence rather than prediction. Since we cannot know the future with certainty, our energy is better invested in developing the qualities that will serve us regardless of what comes: resilience, adaptability, courage, patience, and equanimity.

This approach doesn't mean abandoning planning or preparation. Rather, it means holding our plans lightly, remaining flexible in the face of changing circumstances, and grounding our security in internal qualities rather than external conditions.

A practice I recommend for developing comfort with uncertainty is what I call "planned unpredictability"-deliberately introducing small elements of the unknown into your routine. Take a day trip without planning your itinerary. Attend an event outside your usual interests. Have a conversation without an agenda. These small exercises build the mental flexibility that serves when larger uncertainties arise.

The ultimate teaching of Master Shi Heng Yi on resilience and growth might be summarized in his statement about the warrior monk: "A warrior monk is both a warrior and a monk. Perhaps they are a warrior at their core, but their external behavior is peaceful. They choose to be peaceful and are skillful at peace, but the ability to protect themselves and their loved ones is always present."

This integration of strength and peace, of capacity and choice, emerges only through willingly engaging with challenge rather than avoiding it. The comfort we truly seek isn't the absence of difficulty but the presence of capabilities equal to whatever life presents. This is the promise of embracing discomfort-not a life without challenges, but a self equal to them.

As we conclude this exploration of character and virtue, remember that the qualities we've discussed aren't abstract ideals but practical capacities developed through consistent practice. The Shaolin virtues, lived with integrity and strengthened through challenge, form not just the foundation of self-mastery but of a life of meaning, impact, and genuine fulfillment.

Notes

Day:
Date & Month:

V

Living with Purpose, Peace, and Ongoing Growth

Integrate all lessons to live with deeper purpose and peace. Embrace letting go, daily routines for balance, and lifelong learning. Become your own master by sustaining self-mastery in every aspect of life

.

13

Purpose and Meaning-Finding Your Path

The question of purpose haunts many of us throughout our lives. In my years moving between corporate boardrooms and monastery meditation halls, I've heard countless variations of the same fundamental inquiry: "What am I meant to do with my life?" This question takes different forms across life stages-the recent graduate wondering which career to pursue, the mid-life professional questioning if their achievements have meaning, the retiree seeking purpose beyond work-but the underlying longing remains the same.

What struck me most powerfully about Master Shi Heng Yi's teachings on purpose is how they transcend the Western fixation on doing and achievement. "I am not searching for happiness," he explains. "I'm searching for peace." This seemingly simple statement contains revolutionary wisdom about how we might approach the question of purpose and meaning.

The Difference Between Doing and Being

Most of us have been conditioned to define ourselves by what we do-our career, achievements, roles, and responsibilities. We believe purpose is something to be found through action and accomplishment. Yet Master Shi Heng Yi offers a fundamentally different perspective: true purpose emerges not primarily from what we do but from who we are.

This distinction between doing and being isn't merely philosophical-it has profound practical implications. When we locate our sense of meaning exclusively in doing, we become vulnerable to several traps:

The achievement trap-believing we'll find fulfillment once we reach certain milestones, only to discover that each accomplishment leads to a brief satisfaction followed by the need for something more.

The identity trap-becoming so attached to a particular role or activity that we lose ourselves when circumstances change, whether through career transitions, retirement, health challenges, or other life shifts.

The external validation trap-measuring our worth and purpose by others' recognition or society's definitions of success rather than by our own internal compass.

I experienced these traps firsthand during my corporate career. Despite rising to leadership positions and achieving external markers of success, I found myself increasingly disconnected from any sense of deeper meaning. The doing was impressive on paper but hollow in experience.

It was during a retreat with Master Shi Heng Yi that I began to understand the being dimension of purpose. He shared, "For my son there is nothing to be done. There is nothing he has to achieve. If there would be something, it is stay connected." This insight-that connection rather than achievement might be the essence of purpose-initiated a profound shift in my understanding.

Being doesn't mean passivity or the absence of action. Rather, it

110

refers to the quality of presence, awareness, and authenticity we bring to whatever we do. A teacher fully present with their students, a parent deeply connected with their child, an artist completely absorbed in creation-these expressions of being infuse doing with meaning that transcends measurable outcomes.

The path to purpose begins not with asking "What should I do?" but "How can I be more fully myself?" This question directs attention inward rather than outward, toward essence rather than appearance, toward what Master Shi Heng Yi calls "your source."

Connecting to Your Source and Authentic Self

What exactly is this "source" that Master Shi Heng Yi references? He describes it as "something that is totally untouched, that only you actually know about," a core essence beyond roles, achievements, or others' perceptions. This source isn't something to be created or attained but rather uncovered-it's already there, though often obscured by layers of conditioning, expectation, and habitual patterns.

Connecting to this authentic self requires a journey of both letting go and rediscovery. The practices we've explored throughout this book-from the RAIN method to virtue cultivation to mindfulness training-all serve this deeper purpose of clearing away what isn't essential to reveal what is.

I've guided hundreds of individuals through this process of reconnection, and while each journey is unique, certain approaches consistently help:

Regular periods of silence and solitude-creating space where you can hear your own voice beneath the noise of others' expectations and societal pressures.

Reflection on what brings you alive-not just what you're good at or what earns approval, but what activities, environments, or interactions generate an internal sense of vitality and resonance.

Honest assessment of values-not the values you think you should have or that look good on paper, but what truly matters to you at the deepest level.

Exploration of childhood interests-before the influences of practicality, expectation, or comparison narrowed your expression, what naturally drew your curiosity and enthusiasm?

A client who had built a successful but unfulfilling legal career discovered through these practices that his authentic self was most alive when solving complex problems creatively and helping others navigate difficult transitions. This insight didn't lead him to abandon law entirely but to reshape his practice toward mediation and conflict resolution-a path that honored both his trained skills and his essential nature.

This connection to source becomes the foundation for meaning that transcends particular circumstances. As Master Shi Heng Yi teaches, when you're grounded in your authentic self, purpose isn't something you find once and for all but something you express moment by moment through the quality of your being.

Letting Go of Attachments and Outdated Identities

The journey to authentic purpose inevitably involves releasing what no longer serves-attachments, identities, and patterns that may once have been useful but now constrain your growth and expression.

Master Shi Heng Yi addresses this necessity directly: "It's not about what is it that you possess. It's about what of these possessions are possessing you." This insight applies not just to material possessions but to roles, achievements, beliefs, and identities we cling to beyond their usefulness.

Letting go doesn't happen once but continues throughout life. The identities that served you in your twenties may become limitations in your forties. The beliefs that provided security in one context may prevent growth in another. The goals that once inspired may eventually constrain.

I've found that three questions help facilitate this ongoing process of release:

"What am I holding that is actually holding me?"

"What identity or belief am I defending that's limiting my growth?"

"If I completely let go of how others see me, what would change in how I live?"

These questions often reveal surprising attachments-to being seen as competent, to avoiding vulnerability, to maintaining an image of strength or success, to beliefs about what's possible or appropriate for someone like you.

A senior executive I worked with discovered through this inquiry that his attachment to being the "problem solver" in his organization was preventing both his own development and his team's growth. His identity was so bound up in having answers that he couldn't embrace the deeper leadership needed-creating conditions where others found their own solutions. Letting go of this attachment was painful but ultimately liberating, opening space for both personal renewal and organizational transformation.

The process of letting go creates space for what Master Shi Heng Yi calls "emptiness"-not a nihilistic void but a fertile openness from which authentic purpose can emerge. "I wake up and try to not already have any type of thought from yesterday in my mind," he explains. "I try to wake up empty."

This emptiness doesn't mean abandoning responsibility or commitment. Rather, it means approaching each day, each situation, each relationship with fresh awareness rather than predetermined patterns. From this space of openness, purpose becomes not a fixed destination but a living expression that evolves as you evolve.

The path to purpose is ultimately a journey of integration-bringing together being and doing, inner authenticity and outer expression, personal fulfillment and contribution to something beyond yourself. As Master Shi Heng Yi teaches, true meaning emerges not from achievement alone but from alignment-when who you are flows naturally into what you do, creating a life that feels not merely successful but deeply, authentically yours.

Notes

Day:
Date & Month:

14

Daily Routines for Self-Mastery

"It is the small daily disciplines that build mastery." The last person I expected to hear this wisdom from was the CEO of a Fortune 500 company, yet there he was, describing how his morning meditation practice had transformed not just his leadership but his entire approach to life. What struck me wasn't just his commitment to this practice but how perfectly his experience aligned with Master Shi Heng Yi's teachings on daily routines.

Throughout my years of studying with Master Shi Heng Yi and applying his methods in various contexts, I've found that daily routines are where philosophy meets practice-where lofty ideals about self-mastery become embodied reality. These aren't just good habits but deliberate practices that, performed consistently, reshape our relationship with ourselves and the world.

Morning Silence, Breathwork, and Conscious Presence

Master Shi Heng Yi places special emphasis on how we begin each day: "I wake up and try to not already have any type of thought from yesterday in my mind. I try to wake up empty." This practice of starting with emptiness-with receptivity rather than reactivity-sets the foundation for everything that follows.

The modern morning typically looks quite different: Many of us reach for our phones before our feet touch the floor, immediately filling our minds with others' agendas, news, messages, and demands. We rush through mechanical routines while mentally rehearsing the day ahead or replaying yesterday's events. By the time we arrive at work or begin our main activities, we're already mentally scattered and emotionally reactive.

Master Shi Heng Yi offers an alternative approach that begins with three key practices: silence, breathwork, and conscious presence.

Morning silence doesn't require formal meditation (though that can be valuable). It simply means creating space before engaging with external inputs. This might be five minutes sitting quietly before checking devices, or walking outdoors without music or podcasts, or simply paying full attention to the sensations of your morning shower.

A financier I coached implemented a "digital sunrise" policy-no screens until after breakfast. "Those first 45 minutes now belong to me rather than to the world's demands," he shared. "Everything else flows differently from that foundation."

Breathwork follows naturally from silence. Master Shi Heng Yi describes how conscious breathing helps prepare the body and mind for the day ahead: "You have certain breathing patterns throughout the day. In order to prepare the body, it is all connected with a couple of conscious breathing [practices]."

This doesn't require complex techniques. Simply bringing awareness to your breath for a few minutes-noticing its natural rhythm, perhaps gradually deepening it, feeling the sensations of air entering and leaving your body-activates the parasympathetic nervous system and establishes a state of calm alertness.

Conscious presence builds on this foundation. Rather than moving through morning activities on autopilot, bring full attention to whatever you're doing-whether preparing coffee, getting dressed, or commuting. Notice sensations, observe thoughts without attaching to them, and continually return to the present moment when the mind wanders to past or future.

A physician who incorporated these three practices-silence, breathwork, and conscious presence-reported not only reduced stress but enhanced diagnostic abilities. "When I'm fully present with patients rather than partially distracted by mental noise, I see subtle cues I would have missed before," she explained.

These morning practices don't require significant time investment-even ten or fifteen minutes can create a profound shift in your day. What matters is consistency rather than duration, the regular establishment of a centered state before engaging with external demands.

Standing Meditation and Mindful Exercise

Physical practices form another crucial element of Master Shi Heng Yi's daily routine. He specifically emphasizes standing practice-holding postures that build both physical strength and mental willpower: "I maintain a certain standing thing, for 15 minutes. Standing position means... I'm standing very firm."

This practice might seem strange to those accustomed to movement-based exercise, but standing meditation offers unique benefits. Physically, it strengthens the legs and core, improves posture, and develops stability. Mentally, it builds focus, patience, and the capacity to remain present with discomfort-qualities that transfer to every aspect of life.

A simple standing practice involves standing with feet shoulder-width apart, knees slightly bent, spine straight but not rigid, arms either at your sides or in a gentle "holding the ball" position in front of your chest. Begin with two minutes and gradually extend the duration as capacity increases.

I've guided executives, athletes, and artists in adapting this practice to their needs, often with remarkable results. A corporate leader who implemented daily standing practice reported not only physical benefits but enhanced emotional regulation: "In meetings that would have triggered me before, I now feel the same steadiness I cultivate in my standing practice."

Beyond standing meditation, Master Shi Heng Yi advocates for mindful movement-physical activity performed with full presence rather than distraction. This could be formal practice like tai chi or yoga, or simply bringing mindful awareness to walking, climbing stairs, or other daily movements.

The key quality is complete attention to the physical experience-feeling the sensations of movement, noticing the breath, observing the mind's responses. This integration of awareness and action develops the mind-body unity that characterizes true self-mastery.

A dancer I worked with transformed her training through this approach. Rather than mechanically repeating movements or constantly evaluating her performance, she brought complete presence to each gesture. "My technique actually improved," she reported, "but more importantly, I rediscovered the joy that drew me to dance in the first place."

These physical practices don't require athletic ability or previous training. They're accessible to anyone willing to begin where they are and develop progressively. What matters is not the initial capacity but the quality of presence and the consistency of practice.

Regulating Emotions and Maintaining Peace

The culmination of these daily practices is what Master Shi Heng Yi describes as "being in a state" of peace rather than constantly seeking happiness-a subtle but profound distinction. While happiness depends on external circumstances and inevitably fluctuates, peace represents a more stable condition that can be maintained even amid difficulty or challenge.

Emotional regulation-the ability to work skillfully with emotions rather than being controlled by them-is essential for this peace. Master Shi Heng Yi describes how he approaches this practice: "I tell myself in this situation you will not get angry, you will not hate, because you understand why the other person is like that."

This isn't about suppressing emotions but about responding to them with awareness rather than reactivity. The daily routines we've explored-morning silence, breathwork, standing practice, mindful movement-all build the foundation for this capacity, creating space between stimulus and response.

Specific practices for emotional regulation include:

Naming emotions as they arise-"I notice anger is present" rather than "I am angry."

Physical awareness-noticing how emotions manifest in your body (tension, heat, constriction) and using breath to create space around these sensations.

Perspective shift-stepping back from personal narrative to see the larger context, as Master Shi Heng Yi suggests when he considers why others behave as they do.

A corporate negotiator I coached transformed his effectiveness through these practices. Previously reactive when deals stalled or counterparts made aggressive moves, he learned to recognize emotional triggers and respond from centered awareness rather than defensiveness. "I can still feel the emotion," he shared, "but now there's a space where I can choose my response rather than being driven by reaction."

The ultimate aim of these emotional practices isn't to reach some perfect state of perpetual calm but to develop the capacity to return to peace more quickly when disturbed. Master Shi Heng Yi describes this as an ongoing process: "I think there's more and more peace in your life. But I don't think there's like a state of complete peace."

This realistic approach acknowledges that disturbances will arise-the question is how we relate to them. Through consistent practice of the routines we've explored, we develop the capacity to maintain inner stability amid external fluctuation, to respond rather than react, and to return to center when we inevitably get pulled off balance.

Daily routines might seem small in isolation, but their cumulative effect is transformative. As Master Shi Heng Yi teaches, these aren't just good habits but the very foundation of self-mastery-the bridge between philosophical understanding and lived reality. Through these consistent practices, moment by moment and day by day, we gradually become the person capable of living with authentic purpose and abiding peace.

Notes

Day:
Date & Month:

15

Becoming Your Own Master

During a particularly challenging period in my monastic training, I found myself seeking guidance from every teacher I could access, hoping someone would provide the definitive answers to my struggles. It was then that Master Shi Heng Yi offered perhaps his most important teaching: "Don't rely on a master for him to run your life. This whole journey is about you learning and acquiring the skills and knowledge necessary to bring out the best version of yourself."

This statement captures the essence of self-mastery-not dependence on external authority but the development of your own inner wisdom and capability. Throughout this book, we've explored various aspects of Master Shi Heng Yi's methodology, from understanding hindrances to applying the RAIN method, from cultivating virtues to establishing daily routines. All these teachings point toward the same ultimate goal: becoming your own master.

Self-Reliance and the Master Within

Master Shi Heng Yi's approach differs fundamentally from many spiritual and self-help traditions that position the teacher as an ongoing source of guidance and direction. Instead, he emphasizes that "the master is already sitting inside of each individual. It's just that we don't nourish that master inside of us enough."

This perspective doesn't diminish the value of teachers, mentors, or guides. Rather, it clarifies their proper role-not as permanent authorities to be followed but as temporary supports who help us recognize and develop our own innate wisdom.

I've witnessed both approaches in my work with organizations and individuals. Some leaders create cultures of dependency, where team members constantly seek approval and direction. Others foster self-reliance, helping people develop the judgment and confidence to navigate challenges independently.

The difference in results is striking. Dependent teams collapse in the leader's absence; self-reliant teams thrive. Dependent individuals remain stunted in their growth; self-reliant individuals continue evolving throughout life.

The journey toward self-reliance begins with recognizing your own inherent capacity for wisdom. This doesn't mean you know everything or never need guidance. It means trusting that with proper training and attention, you can develop the discernment to navigate your particular path.

A writer I coached had spent years jumping between creative workshops and mentors, constantly seeking external validation and direction. Through working with Master Shi Heng Yi's principles, she gradually recognized that her excessive seeking actually reflected a lack of trust in her own creative voice. As she began to nourish "the master within"-developing her own aesthetic judgment and creative process-her work gained both authenticity and impact.

This self-reliance doesn't develop overnight but through consistent practice of the methods we've explored throughout this book. The RAIN technique helps you work skillfully with hindrances rather than being controlled by them. Virtue cultivation builds the character framework that supports wise decisions. Daily routines establish the foundation of awareness and presence from which inner wisdom can emerge.

Through these practices, you gradually transition from external direction to internal guidance-not by rejecting teachers but by integrating their wisdom so completely that it becomes your own. As Master Shi Heng Yi often says, "The student should eventually surpass the master."

Not Outsourcing Your Well-Being

A crucial aspect of becoming your own master involves taking full responsibility for your well-being rather than outsourcing it to people or circumstances beyond your control. Master Shi Heng Yi addresses this directly: "Place the emphasis and the foundation of your well-being only on things that you have influence on. And which one is that? Your body and your mind."

This principle stands in stark contrast to how many of us approach well-being. We make our happiness dependent on others' behavior, societal conditions, professional achievements, or material acquisitions. When these external factors align with our preferences, we feel good; when they don't, we suffer-creating a perpetual rollercoaster of emotional reactivity.

The alternative is placing the foundation of your well-being on what you can actually influence-your responses, perspectives, habits, and practices. This doesn't mean denying the impact of external circumstances or attempting to control everything. Rather, it means focusing your energy on your sphere of influence rather than your sphere of concern.

I've guided numerous individuals through this shift in emphasis, often with transformative results. A healthcare professional struggling with pandemic-related burnout was focusing primarily on systemic failures beyond her control-administrative decisions, resource shortages, political responses. While these concerns were valid, her exclusive focus on them left her feeling helpless and depleted.

Through applying Master Shi Heng Yi's teaching, she redirected attention to her sphere of influence: her breathing practices, her ability to be fully present with each patient, her capacity to find meaning even in difficult circumstances. This shift didn't change the external challenges but transformed her relationship to them, restoring a sense of agency and purpose amid ongoing difficulty.

Not outsourcing your well-being requires consistent vigilance. Our habitual tendency is to attribute our internal states to external causes: "The traffic made me angry" rather than "I responded to the traffic with anger" or "Her comment hurt me" rather than "I felt hurt in response to her comment."

These subtle linguistic shifts reflect a profound difference in orientation-from seeing yourself as passive recipient of circumstances to recognizing yourself as an active responder with choice about how you engage with whatever arises.

Master Shi Heng Yi models this responsibility through his own approach to life's challenges: "When they dislike, that's not my problem. I'm not suffering from the fact that someone dislikes [me]. I'm only concerned with what is right." This isn't indifference to others but a clear discernment between what we can and cannot control.

Taking responsibility for your well-being doesn't guarantee constant happiness or freedom from pain. Life inevitably includes difficulty and challenge. The difference lies in how you relate to these experiences-as defining impositions that determine your state or as opportunities to practice the skills of self-mastery you've been developing.

Lifelong Learning, Refinement, and the Pursuit of Peace

Becoming your own master isn't a destination but a continuous journey of learning, refinement, and deepening. Master Shi Heng Yi emphasizes that this pursuit never ends: "I think there's more and more peace in your life. But I don't think there's like a state of complete peace."

This perspective liberates us from the perfectionist trap that derails many spiritual and personal development journeys. The goal isn't to reach some ideal state where challenges never arise, mistakes never occur, or growth is no longer needed. Rather, it's to develop the capacity for ongoing learning and refinement-to become increasingly skillful in navigating life's complexity.

I've observed how this orientation toward lifelong learning distinguishes those who sustain growth from those who eventually plateau or regress. The former maintain humility and curiosity regardless of their achievements; the latter become rigid in their certainty, resistant to new information that might challenge established patterns.

A senior meditation teacher I worked with embodied this principle beautifully. Despite decades of practice and widespread recognition, he approached each day with the beginner's mind that Master Shi Heng Yi advocates-empty of yesterday's conclusions, open to fresh discovery. "The moment I think I've arrived," he shared, "is the moment my practice becomes stale."

This ongoing refinement applies across all dimensions of self-mastery:

In understanding hindrances, you continually deepen your recognition of how they manifest in increasingly subtle forms.

In virtue development, you refine the expression of qualities like

129

patience or courage across ever more challenging contexts.

In daily routines, you don't just repeat practices but bring fresh attention to each engagement, discovering new layers of awareness and capacity.

The pursuit of peace that Master Shi Heng Yi emphasizes differs fundamentally from the pursuit of happiness that drives much of modern life. While happiness depends on favorable conditions and pleasurable experiences, peace emerges from right relationship with whatever arises-pleasant or unpleasant, easy or difficult.

This doesn't mean rejecting happiness when it naturally occurs but recognizing its inherently transient nature. As Master Shi Heng Yi notes, "Happiness and sadness, they come always in a pair." Peace, by contrast, can be present even amid challenge or discomfort-not as an emotion but as a quality of being.

The journey toward this peace isn't separate from ordinary life but emerges through it. Each interaction, challenge, or experience becomes an opportunity for practice-for applying the methods we've explored and refining your capacity to embody them naturally.

A business leader who incorporated Master Shi Heng Yi's teachings into her approach described this integration beautifully: "I used to compartmentalize-meditation was meditation, work was work, relationships were relationships. Now I see it's all one practice-bringing the same quality of awareness and intention to everything I do."

This integrated approach represents the essence of becoming your own master-not achieving some externally defined pinnacle but developing the internal resources to navigate your particular path with wisdom, resilience, and peace. The journey doesn't end; it continues to unfold, offering endless opportunities for learning, refinement, and growth.

As Master Shi Heng Yi teaches, "Don't rely on theories in the book. Go out there, experiment with it and see if that's something that's going to be useful on your own path." The teachings and practices we've explored aren't dogma to be accepted but tools to be tested, refined, and ultimately made your own.

Notes

Day:
Date & Month:

16

Real-Life Applications and Stories

Throughout this book, we've explored the principles and practices of Master Shi Heng Yi's approach to self-mastery. Now we turn to perhaps the most compelling evidence of their power: the real-life transformations they've catalyzed across diverse contexts and circumstances.

As I've applied these methods in corporate settings, educational institutions, healthcare environments, and one-on-one coaching relationships, I've witnessed remarkable shifts-not just in external circumstances but in the fundamental relationship people have with themselves and their lives. These stories aren't exceptions or anomalies but natural outcomes of the consistent application of the principles we've explored.

Case Studies and Stories of Transformation

From Reactive Leader to Centered Presence

Michael, a technology executive with a reputation for brilliant strategy but volatile emotions, found himself at a crossroads when a 360-degree review revealed that his reactivity was undermining his effectiveness. Team members described walking on eggshells, withholding information for fear of triggering his anger, and feeling drained by the emotional intensity he brought to interactions.

Through applying the RAIN method to work with his emotional triggers, developing a standing practice for regulation, and systematically cultivating the virtue of patience, Michael transformed his leadership. Six months into this work, a team member remarked, "It's like working with a different person-he still has high standards, but now there's a steadiness and presence that makes it safe to bring our best thinking."

The key insight for Michael came through recognizing how aversion-the second hindrance-was driving his reactions. Whenever faced with obstacles or others' perceived incompetence, he would reflexively push away the discomfort through anger or control. By learning to stay present with this discomfort rather than immediately reacting, he discovered a capacity for creative response rather than habitual reaction.

From Chronic Indecision to Clear Direction

Sarah, a talented writer and artist, had struggled for years with what she initially described as "creative block" but gradually recognized as the hindrance of doubt. Despite significant talent and opportunities, she repeatedly abandoned projects before completion, second-guessed her decisions, and sought endless input from others rather than trusting her own voice.

Through working with the Five Hindrances framework and developing daily routines that connected her to her "source," Sarah gradually transformed her relationship with doubt. Rather than being paralyzed by it, she learned to recognize doubt as a mental state rather than reality-a cloud passing through awareness rather than the sky itself.

A pivotal moment came when she applied the principle of "becoming your own master" to her creative process. Instead of constantly seeking external validation, she developed the practice of sitting in silence before beginning work, connecting to her own aesthetic judgment and creative instincts. Within a year, she had completed her first book manuscript after a decade of false starts.

From Achievement Addiction to Meaningful Contribution

James, a successful entrepreneur who had built and sold multiple companies, sought coaching not for professional challenges but for what he described as "an emptiness that no achievement seems to fill." Despite external success, he felt increasingly disconnected from any sense of meaning or purpose.

Through exploring Master Shi Heng Yi's distinction between doing and being, James began to recognize how his identity had become fused with achievement. His worth and purpose were entirely defined by what he accomplished rather than who he was, creating an insatiable need for the next success to maintain his sense of self.

The transformation began with simple daily practices-morning silence, conscious breathing, and standing meditation-that gradually helped him recognize a dimension of himself beyond accomplishment. As this awareness deepened, he naturally shifted from achievement-driven action to purpose-guided contribution, eventually founding an organization that combined his business expertise with genuine service to underresourced entrepreneurs.

From Chronic Stress to Sustainable Well-Being

Elena, a physician working in a high-pressure hospital environment, was experiencing classic burnout symptoms-exhaustion, cynicism, and reduced efficacy. Despite loving medicine, she found herself increasingly numb to both her patients' needs and her own well-being.

Through implementing Master Shi Heng Yi's teaching on "not outsourcing your well-being," Elena shifted from focusing primarily on external conditions (administrative demands, patient volume, systemic challenges) to developing internal resources (emotional regulation, present-moment awareness, physical restoration).

A key practice for Elena became what she called "threshold moments"- brief pauses before entering each patient's room to release the previous interaction and return to centered presence. These micro-practices, combined with a morning routine of silence and breathwork, gradually rebuilt her resilience and reconnected her to the purpose that had initially drawn her to medicine.

Exercises and Reflection Prompts for Each Chapter

The transformations described above didn't occur through passive reading but through active engagement with practices and principles. Here, we offer specific exercises corresponding to each part of this book, designed to translate understanding into lived experience.

Part 1: The Foundations of Self-Mastery

Reflection: Identify one area where you consistently feel stuck or dissatisfied. How might the modern struggles described in Chapter 1 (choice overload, disconnection from body, autopilot living) be contributing to this challenge?

Practice: For one week, create a daily "director's moment"-a brief period where you step back from immersion in your life's movie and consciously consider: What story am I currently living? Is this the story I want to write? How might I direct this scene differently?

Part 2: The Five Hindrances-Identifying Your Inner Obstacles

Reflection: Which of the five hindrances most frequently affects your progress toward important goals? What triggers tend to activate this hindrance for you?

Practice: Select one recurring situation where hindrances typically arise (such as a challenging work task, difficult conversation, or personal discipline). For the next five instances of this situation, pause before engaging and ask: Is a hindrance present right now? Which one? How is it manifesting in my body and mind?

Part 3: Tools and Practices for Transformation

Reflection: Consider a pattern that consistently undermines your well-being or effectiveness. Using the RAIN method, how might you approach this pattern differently?

Practice: Develop a "minimum viable commitment" for mind-body training-a brief daily practice that integrates physical and mental elements. This might be a five-minute standing meditation, a conscious walking practice, or mindful movement combined with breathwork.

Part 4: Building Character and Virtue

Reflection: Which of the Shaolin virtues feels most developed in your life? Which would benefit from conscious cultivation? How might strengthening this virtue affect your current challenges?

Practice: Select one virtue to focus on for 30 days. Each morning, set a specific intention for how you'll express this virtue today. Each evening, reflect on opportunities, successes, and learning edges in your practice.

Part 5: Living with Purpose, Peace, and Ongoing Growth

Reflection: Where in your life might you be outsourcing your well-being to factors beyond your control? How could you redirect energy toward your sphere of influence?

Practice: Design a morning routine incorporating elements of Master Shi Heng Yi's approach: silence, breathwork, conscious presence, and some form of standing or movement practice. Experiment with this routine for at least two weeks, noting shifts in your state and capabilities.

Creating Your Personal Mastery Plan

While the exercises above offer entry points for engaging with specific aspects of Master Shi Heng Yi's teachings, sustainable transformation emerges from a comprehensive approach tailored to your unique circumstances and aspirations. The following framework helps translate these teachings into a personalized plan for ongoing development.

Step 1: Honest Assessment

Begin by assessing your current state across multiple dimensions:

Physical body: Energy, strength, flexibility, resilience

Mental clarity: Focus, presence, cognitive function

Emotional landscape: Regulation, awareness, balance

Relational quality: Connection, communication, boundaries

Ethical framework: Alignment between values and actions

Spiritual dimension: Purpose, meaning, transpersonal connection

For each dimension, note both strengths to build upon and opportunities for growth.

Step 2: Priority Identification

Based on your assessment, identify 2-3 priority areas for initial focus. Rather than attempting transformation across all dimensions simultaneously, strategic focus creates momentum that eventually extends to other areas.

Consider both urgency (what needs immediate attention) and leverage (what improvements would positively affect multiple dimensions).

Step 3: Practice Selection

For each priority area, select specific practices from Master Shi Heng Yi's methodology:

For working with hindrances, apply the RAIN method to specific triggering situations.

For building virtues, design targeted challenges that stretch your capacity in measured ways.

For mind-body integration, incorporate standing practice, conscious breathing, or mindful movement.

For connecting to source, establish regular periods of silence and self-reflection.

Step 4: Implementation Structure

Create a sustainable structure for implementation, considering:

Daily practices: What will you engage with every day, even briefly?

Weekly practices: What requires more extended time and might be scheduled weekly?

Environmental supports: How will you design your physical and social environment to support your practice?

Accountability measures: How will you track progress and maintain commitment?

Step 5: Review and Refinement

Establish regular intervals for reviewing your practice and refining your approach:

Daily: Brief noting of insights, challenges, or shifts

Weekly: More extensive reflection on patterns and adjustments needed

Monthly: Comprehensive review of progress and plan refinement

Quarterly: Reassessment across all dimensions, with potential reprioritization

This ongoing cycle of practice, reflection, and refinement embodies Master Shi Heng Yi's teaching that self-mastery is not a destination but a lifelong journey of learning and development.

As we conclude this exploration of Master Shi Heng Yi's methodology, remember his essential teaching: "The master is already sitting inside of each individual. It's just that we don't nourish that master inside of us enough." The practices and principles we've explored throughout this book offer pathways for this nourishment-not as abstract theories but as lived experiences that gradually transform your relationship with yourself and the world.

The journey of self-mastery unfolds one moment, one breath, one choice at a time. It doesn't demand dramatic upheaval but rather consistent attention to how you show up in ordinary circumstances. Through this attention-this nourishing of the master within-you gradually become more fully yourself: more present, more capable, more at peace amid life's inevitable challenges and opportunities.

Notes

Day:
Date & Month:

17

Conclusion

As we reach the end of our journey through Master Shi Heng Yi's teachings, it's important to recognize that this conclusion is not truly an ending, but rather a transition point in your ongoing path of self-mastery.

Throughout this book, we've explored the foundations of self-awareness, examined the five hindrances that block our progress, learned practical tools like the RAIN method, cultivated virtue and character, and discovered ways to live with greater purpose and peace. Yet the true value of these teachings lies not in understanding them intellectually, but in applying them consistently to your daily life.

Master Shi Heng Yi reminds us that "the master is already sitting inside of each individual. It's just that we don't nourish that master inside of us enough." This simple yet profound insight captures the essence of self-mastery-not as something to be acquired from outside yourself, but as an innate capacity waiting to be recognized, developed, and expressed.

As you move forward from these pages, remember that self-mastery is not about achieving perfection or eliminating all challenges. It's about developing the awareness, discipline, and wisdom to navigate life's inevitable ups and downs with greater skill and equanimity. It's about placing the foundation of your well-being on what you can actually influence-your body and mind-rather than outsourcing it to external circumstances beyond your control.

The practices we've explored-from morning silence to standing meditation, from virtue cultivation to the RAIN method-are not ends in themselves but vehicles for awakening the master within. They are bridges between understanding and embodiment, between knowing and being.

Whatever challenges you face as you continue your journey, remember to ask yourself: What is blocking me right now? What hindrance is at work? What virtue needs strengthening? What pattern needs breaking? Then invest your energy in addressing that specific obstacle, one step at a time.

The path of self-mastery unfolds differently for each person. Your journey will have its own unique rhythm, challenges, and break-throughs. Trust this process. Be patient with yourself. Celebrate small victories. Learn from setbacks. And above all, maintain that quality of persistence that Master Shi Heng Yi emphasizes-the willingness to get up and try again, regardless of how many times you fall.

May the teachings in this book serve as both mirror and map-reflecting your own inner wisdom while providing practical guidance for the path ahead. And may your journey of self-mastery bring not only personal fulfillment but also benefit to all whose lives you touch.

The journey continues, one breath, one choice, one moment at a time.

Printed in Dunstable, United Kingdom